Cloud of Witnesses
Ancient Stories of Faith

Berean Study Series

Cloud of Witnesses: Ancient Stories of Faith
Published by Heritage Christian University Press

Copyright © 2020 by Ed Gallagher

Manufactured in the United States of America

Cataloging-in-Publication Data
Cloud of witnesses: ancient stories of faith / edited by Ed Gallagher
Berean study series
p. cm.
Includes Scripture index.
ISBN 978-1-7347665-0-9 (pbk.)
1. Bible. Hebrews—Study and teaching.
I. Gallagher, Edmon L. II. Title. III. Series.
BS2775 .C57 2020   227.87007—dc20 2020-941233

Cover design by Brittany Vander Maas and Brad McKinnon

All rights reserved. No part of this publication may be reproduced, distributed, stored in a retrieval system, or transmitted in any form or by any means without the prior written permission of the publisher, except in the case of brief quotations embodied in critical reviews and certain other noncommercial uses permitted by copyright law.

Copyright permission in credits

Contents

1	By Faith	
	Ed Gallagher	3
2	Enoch	
	Jeffrey Brothers	13
3	Noah	
	Brad McKinnon	19
4	Abraham	
	Michael Jackson	26
5	Sarah	
	Justin Guin	35
6	Joseph	
	Nathan Daily	43
7	Moses	
	C. Wayne Kilpatrick	52
8	Rahab	
	Kirk Brothers	59

9	Barak	
	Arvy Dupuy	67
10	Gideon	
	Philip Goad	74
11	Sawn in Two	
	Jeremy W. Barrier	81
12	Samson	
	Travis Harmon	87
13	Samuel	
	Nathan Guy	93
	Scripture Index	102
	Contributors	108
	Credits	110

Cloud of Witnesses

By Faith
Ed Gallagher

Focus Passage: Hebrews 11:1
One Main Thing: Faith is the foundation of our lives, directed toward a hoped-for future, trusting in the God who rewards believers.

Introduction

So, Dory looks at Marlin and says, "He says it's time to let go." Of course, Marlin doesn't believe her; not only is Marlin a naturally anxious fish, always worried about danger, but he's also learned that Dory is a fish that can't always be trusted. She's got … issues. But in this predicament, inside a whale's mouth and holding on for dear life, Dory insists that she can understand the whale's speech, and she knows what they ought to do. They ought to let go. Marlin reluctantly acquiesces, and it turns out that Dory was right. Now, certainly, that scene in *Finding Nemo* is about overcoming anxiety, a good biblical theme (Matt 6:25–34), but it's also about trust. Marlin needed to trust Dory, trust that she had information that he didn't have (because she could speak whale), trust that her advice would result in success. It's a major theme of the movie, fear vs. faith, even faith in this hopelessly—well, not quite hopelessly—forgetful fish. Earlier, Dory had told Marlin that they needed to swim through a particular trench, not over it, advice to which Marlin strongly objected. Dory pleaded, "Come on, trust me on this." Marlin was incredulous: "Trust you?" Dory replied, "Yes, trust—it's what friends do." Here again, Marlin's trust, his faith, in Dory would have been well-placed, because Dory knew more about this trench than Marlin did.

Faith is about trust. It's about confidence in yourself or someone else. When I was a kid (and still pretty much today), I had complete confidence in my dad in a lot of situations. I knew if there was a problem, my dad would be able to solve it. Or, when it snowed in our southern town, I remember my dad wanting to get out and drive around town, see the blanket of white all over town, observe all the closed schools and businesses. Some people would have been nervous to drive in the snow, but not my dad, and I was not at all nervous about riding with him. I had confidence in him. I had faith that he could drive in snow.

God wants us to have faith in him. By some amazing circumstance—actually, we should call it amazing grace—that's pretty much all God wants from us. He knows we're not very bright, not very talented, pretty incompetent at most things. He doesn't expect much from us—just trust, faith, confidence in him. Of course, that means that when he tells us to do something, he expects us to trust him enough to do it. But it's not like he's told us to come up with a plan for saving the world. It's not like he expects us to do anything perfectly, or even very well. And let me say that you could get no better list of people who did not do things perfectly than the Faith Hall of Fame roll call in Hebrews 11. Nevertheless, these people show us faith. That's the whole point.

In fact, faith is such a defining element of what it means to be a Christian that one of the most common ways of referring to Christians in the New Testament is "believers."[1]

Going Deeper

How about some statistics? The Greek word for "faith" is *pistis* (πίστις), which appears 243 times in the New Testament. But that's just the noun. The verb "I believe" is *pisteuō* (πιστεύω), appearing 241 times in the New Testament, and the adjective "faithful" (*pistos*, πιστός) appears another sixty-seven times. If you're looking for these words in the New Testament, it probably won't surprise you that you should turn to Romans, which uses the noun forty times and the verb twenty-one times; and John, which uses the verb ninety-eight times (but never the noun); and Acts, which uses the noun fifteen times and the verb thirty-seven times.

As for Hebrews,[2] the noun *pistis* appears thirty-two times, of which twenty-four are in chapter 11.[3] Hebrews uses the verb *pisteuō* only twice (4:3; 11:6), and the adjective *pistos* five times (2:17; 3:2, 5; 10:23; 11:11).

---

[1] For an exploration of the use of "believers" for Christians in the New Testament, see Paul Trebilco, *Self-Designations and Group Identity in the New Testament* (Cambridge: Cambridge University Press, 2012), ch. 3.

[2] Dennis R. Lindsay, "*Pistis* and *'Emunah*: The Nature of Faith in the Epistle to the Hebrews," in *A Cloud of Witnesses: The Theology of Hebrews in Its Ancient Contexts*, ed. Richard Bauckham, et al. (London: T&T Clark, 2008), 158–69, especially 160–61.

[3] The eight appearances of *pistis* in Hebrews outside chapter 11 are at 4:2; 6:1, 12; 10:22, 38, 39; 12:2; 13:7.

Let me bring in one more element before moving off of statistics. The Hebrew word most often associated with faith is *emunah*, which appears most famously in Habakkuk 2:4 (where the Greek translation, the Septuagint, has *pistis*), the verse quoted immediately before the Faith Hall of Fame chapter (Hebrews 10:38). The other famous "faith" verse in the Old Testament is Genesis 15:6, where the verbal form of *emunah* is used (and the Septuagint has *pisteuō*).

Oh, yeah, and one more thing: the single word *pistis* can cover all of the English words "faith" and "belief" and "faithfulness," all of which carry slightly different nuances in English.[4]

What do these words mean?[5] Hebrews provides us with a definition, sort of. One of the problems is that Hebrews 11:1 is notoriously difficult to translate. Here are some options.

> Now faith is the substance of things hoped for, the evidence of things not seen. (KJV)
>
> Now faith is confidence in what we hope for and assurance about what we do not see. (NIV)
>
> Now faith is the assurance of things hoped for, the conviction of things not seen. (NASB, ESV)

---

[4] For a discussion focused on the translation "faithfulness," see Matthew W. Bates, *Gospel Allegiance: What Faith in Jesus Misses for Salvation in Christ* (Grand Rapids: Brazos, 2019), ch. 2. Bates prefers "loyalty" or "allegiance" to "faithfulness" as a translation of *pistis*.

[5] The authoritative work here is Teresa Morgan, *Roman Faith and Christian Faith: Pistis and Fides in the Early Roman Empire and Early Churches* (Oxford: Oxford University Press, 2015). Morgan discusses Hebrews on pp. 330–41. See also Nijay K. Gupta, *Paul and the Language of Faith* (Grand Rapids: Eerdmans, 2020).

Now faith is the reality of what is hoped for, the proof of what is not seen. (CSB)

As you can tell, the translation issues really revolve around two words, which we can give in their Greek form this way.

Now faith is the *hypostasis* (ὑπόστασις) of things hoped for, the *elenchos* (ἔλεγχος) of things not seen.

These words—*hypostasis* and *elenchos*—are not rare in Greek; it's the opposite problem: they occur quite a bit, with a range of meanings, so the difficulty is knowing which of their meanings is at play in our verse. Of course, we're not going to explore the meanings of these words in detail here, but we can take note of some recent discussions of them.

Teresa Morgan argues that *hypostasis* is best translated "foundation" here. According to Morgan, faith is foundational in that it creates our relationship with God (i.e. it is the foundation of our relationship). Faith is the foundation of things hoped for: it is the reason we can hope to achieve these things. As for the second half of the verse and the meaning of *elenchos*, "the likeliest meanings (which are all closely related to one another) are 'evidence', 'proof', or 'test'."[6] Morgan translates: faith is "the proof of everything (which God has promised) that [we] have not yet seen."[7] God has made promises to us about things that lie in the future—we have not yet seen them. Through faith, "we come to prove the reality of

---

[6] Morgan, *Roman Faith and Christian Faith*, 338–41.
[7] Morgan, *Roman Faith and Christian Faith*, 340.

what God has promised us and we hope for but have not yet seen: eternal life."

According to Nijay Gupta, "faith" in Hebrews 11:1 is a kind of spiritual sight,

> a kind of divinely enabled extrasensory perception, a second way of seeing and knowing. One can have confidence in what appears invisible—not because it is mere hunch or opinion, but because he or she has been given access to a perceptual key that unlocks a divine reality.[8]

And, of course, that key is faith, the trust that God knows things we don't know, has power we don't have, and loves us (i.e., exactly in accordance with Hebrews 11:6). So also, Matthew Bates interprets faith here as "a willingness to act on God's more certain underlying reality (*hypostasis*) that is invisible yet visible through the manifestation of God's revealed word."[9]

The main point—a point we can get from this verse whether or not we know the precise nuances of each word—is that our faith is directed toward God, acknowledging that there are things for which we hope, things we cannot see, and yet we trust God, and such trust leads us to action.

That seems all very abstract. What does such faith look like in practice? That's what Hebrews 11 is all about. Such faith looks like Enoch and Noah and Abraham and Sarah and Moses and Rahab and Samuel. Most of all, it looks like Jesus (Heb 12:2). What

---

[8] Gupta, *Paul and the Language of Faith*, 10. See also Bates, *Gospel Allegiance*, 60, who denies that our verse promotes faith without evidence.
[9] Bates, *Gospel Allegiance*, 254–55n3.

all these examples show us is that *pistis* in Hebrews 11 includes trust, faithfulness, belief, confidence, obedience, and hope.[10]

Application

The writer of Hebrews isn't just trying to fill out a certain number of pages; that's not why he goes through this list of examples. He's trying to motivate his readers to endure, to maintain their faith. These readers had apparently been Christians for a while, long enough that the writer now reminds them of the early days of their faith and how fervent their faith was (Hebrews 10:32). Back then, they endured persecution and had compassion on the oppressed (10:33–34). Now, perhaps, it was a different story, so that the writer admonishes, "you need endurance" (10:36). He reminds them of the things in which they hope, the promises of God (10:36), and then he quotes Habakkuk 2:3–4 (as Paul also does: Romans 1:17; Galatians 3:11).

> For yet in a very little while
> the one who is coming will come and will not delay;
> but my righteous one will live by faith.
> My soul takes no pleasure in anyone who shrinks back.

Our writer affirms: "But we are not among those who shrink back and so are lost, but among those who have faith and so are saved" (10:39).

In this way, the writer of Hebrews introduces his sustained reflection on the nature of faith, through illustrations of people who did not shrink back. These people were asked to do,

---

[10] Morgan, *Roman Faith and Christian Faith*, 335.

sometimes crazy things, and they did not shrink back. They faced hardship, and they did not shrink back. "All these died in faith without having received the promises, but from a distance they saw and greeted them" (11:13). We stand in the same position, looking forward to the promises, the things unseen, and refusing to shrink back.

Or is that too optimistic? Perhaps it would be more realistic to say that faith is disappearing all around us, that shrinking back is exactly what we are good at. Maybe when we reflect on what God wants us to do—the love and compassion and hope and joy and faithfulness that he wants us to demonstrate—we shrink back in fear and frustration, confident that we cannot possibly do such things.

Then, brethren, we need Hebrews 11. We need to read again the example of Rahab. We need to consider again the life of Samuel. We need to think about what Gideon was up against, and what he was able to accomplish "by faith." And most of all, we need to look to Jesus (Hebrews 12:2), as the writer of Hebrews emphasizes time and again.[11] There are other examples of faith in Scripture, as well—more mundane examples, less divine, less perfect, and the writer of Hebrews also highlights their faith so that they, too, can serve as examples to us. But Hebrews doesn't really stress the faith of Barak or Rahab or Gideon or Enoch or even Abraham or Moses. These characters are mentioned here and there as

---

[11] Todd D. Still, "Christos as *Pistos*: The Faith(fulness) of Jesus in the Epistle to the Hebrews," in *Cloud of Witnesses*, ed. Richard Bauckham, et al. (London: T & T Clark, 2008), 40–50.

examples of faith, but Jesus is everywhere. If you want to know about faith, look to Jesus.

Conclusion

Hebrews 11 encourages us not just to think about faith in the abstract but as something that must be enacted. That's the point of the great roll call of faith. Look what faith led Enoch to accomplish! And Sarah and Moses and the rest! You can see it when someone trusts God, because their actions provide the evidence. We would not say that Marlin trusted Dori if he had not let go of that whale's tongue. We would not say that Joshua trusted God if he had not led the Israelites around the walls of Jericho for seven days (Hebrews 11:30). We would not say that David trusted God if he cowered in fear before the giant like King Saul and the rest of the Israelites (11:32; 1 Sam 17).

Trust God.

Discussion Questions

1. When you think about faith, what biblical passages immediately come to mind aside from Hebrews 11? (Possibilities: Rom 4; Gal 3; Gen 15:6; John 3:16.) What do each of these passages illustrate about faith?
2. Read Hebrews 11:1 in different translations. How do the different translation options affect the interpretation of the verse? What do all the translation options have in common?
3. What does faith have to do with the future, with things hoped for, with things not seen? In what ways does that aspect of faith make faithfulness more difficult?

4. How does the end of Hebrews 10 work as an introduction to Hebrews 11? What is it that the author of Hebrews is trying to accomplish through this review of the Old Testament heroes of faith?

Enoch

Jeffrey Brothers

Focus Passage: Hebrews 11:5
One main thing: Walk with God to not taste death.

Introduction
>   Genesis 5:21–24
>> When Enoch had lived 65 years, he became the father of Methuselah. And after he became the father of Methuselah, Enoch walked with God 300 years and had other sons and daughters. Altogether Enoch lived 365 years. Enoch walked with God; then he was no more, because God took him away.
>
>   How does an individual walk with God?
>   Genesis 6:5–9
>> The Lord saw how great man's wickedness on the earth had become, and that every inclination of the thoughts of his heart was only evil all the time. The Lord was grieved that he had made man on the earth, and his heart was filled with pain. So the Lord said, "I will wipe mankind, whom I have created from the face of the earth—men and animals, and creatures that move along the ground, and birds of the air—for I am grieved that I have made them." But Noah found favor in the eyes of the Lord. This is the account of Noah. Noah was a righteous man, blameless among the people of his time, and he walked with God.
>
>   How is one commended by God, to be pleasing in God's sight?

This greatly has to do with being blameless among the generation in which we live. In a time when people follow ungodly desires, in a time when the majority has turned away from God, in a time when the inclinations of people's hearts are evil all around the world, this is the time to be set apart by following the desires of a Holy God who has imparted His Spirit so that we may do so. Being blameless and one who walks with God in a generation like this means turning to God for a new heart, with new inclinations and expressions that come from the Spirit of God within.

Enoch was one who was righteous in his time and was considered to be pleasing to the Lord. Surely, he was set apart from the ungodliness of the time in which he lived, in order to speak against it.

Let's look at what we know from the Scriptures about the life of Enoch.

Going Deeper

> Enoch, the seventh from Adam , prophesied about these men: "See, the Lord is coming with thousands upon thousands of his holy ones to judge everyone, and to convict all the ungodly acts they have done in the ungodly way, and of all the harsh words ungodly sinners have spoken against him" (Jude 14).

Jude gives us a little more context about the type of people about whom Enoch prophesied.

³Dear friends, although I was very eager to write to you about the salvation we share, I felt I had to write and urge you to contend for the faith that was once for all entrusted to the saints. ⁴For certain men whose condemnation was written about long ago have secretly slipped in among you. They are godless men, who change the grace of our God into a license for immorality and deny Jesus Christ our only sovereign and Lord. ⁵Though you already know all this, I want to remind you that the Lord delivered his people out of Egypt, but later destroyed those who did not believe. ⁶And the angels who did not keep their positions of authority but abandoned their own home—these he has kept in darkness, bound with everlasting chains for judgment on that great day. ⁷In a similar way, Sodom and Gomorrah and the surrounding towns gave themselves up to sexual immorality and perversion. They serve as an example of those who suffer the punishment of eternal fire. ⁸In the very same way, these dreamers pollute their own bodies, reject authority and slander celestial beings. ⁹But even the archangel Michael, when he was disputing with the devil about the body of Moses, did not dare to bring a slanderous accusation against him, but said, "The Lord rebuke you!" ¹⁰Yet these men speak abusively against whatever they do not understand; and what things they do understand by instinct, like unreasoning animals—these are the very things that destroy them. ¹¹Woe to them! They have taken the way of Cain; they have rushed for profit into Balaam's error; they have been destroyed in Korah's

rebellion. ¹²These men are blemishes at you love feasts, eating with you without the slightest qualm—shepherds who feed only themselves. They are clouds without rain, blown along by the wind; autumn trees, without fruit and uprooted—twice dead. ¹³They are wild waves of the sea, foaming up their shame; wandering stars, for whom blackest darkness has been reserved forever (Jude 3-13).

These men are grumblers and faultfinders; they follow their own evil desires; they boast about themselves and flatter others for their own advantage (Jude 16).

These are the men who divide you, who follow mere natural instincts and do not have the Spirit (Jude 19).

The Way of Cain

As we all know, as a result of disobeying God, Adam and Eve were punished, and part of this punishment was that the ground was cursed (Genesis 3:17). Adam and Eve were not cursed, but the ground from which they were made was cursed and one day will be destroyed. This is where I want to use Cain and his life as a metaphor and an example of prophesies yet to be fulfilled regarding the punishment of that which is cursed—a prophesy of which Enoch spoke. Cain made a living by tilling a cursed ground. Cain labored and toiled in the curse, and even offered God some of what came out of the curse. I am not saying that farmers then or today are like Cain choosing a curse. I emphasize now that I use Cain as a metaphor that is greater than one particular person. But this is the state of the nations. Many have chosen to center their lives around false gods, evil desires, and things that are dedicated to one day being destroyed. Cain lived in the curse, became consumed by the curse, and ultimately took his own brother's life. After this, God cursed Cain, and sometime later Cain would ironically have a son named Enoch (different than the father of Methuselah) and named a city after him, calling it Enoch as well (Genesis 4:17).

Application
God said to his people in Deuteronomy 30,
> [15]See, I set before you today life and prosperity, death and destruction. For I command you today to love the Lord your God, to walk in His ways, and to keep his commands, decrees and laws; then you will live and increase in the land you are entering to possess. ... [19]This day I call heaven and earth as witnesses against you that I have set before you life and death, blessings and curses. Now choose life, so that you and your children may live.

Take no part in cursed things. Take no part in things set for a time of destruction. Take no part in that which leads to death. On the contrary, be blameless in this generation and walk with God. Be set apart from the ways of those who have turned from God. Speak the word of truth and prophesy as one who walks with God, as Enoch did, and you will not taste of death.

Conclusion
> By faith Enoch was taken from this life, so that he did not experience death; he could not be found because God had taken him away. For before he was taken, he was commended as one

who pleased God. Enoch had the faith to speak the word of God in a corrupt generation. He had the faith to speak of the coming destruction of all those who are ungodly and those who take the way of Cain. As a result of this kind of faith, Enoch did not see death, but was taken by God.

Discussion

1. What evidence does the world around you have that shows your walk with God?
2. Are you currently taking the way of Cain?
3. How do your thoughts, your speech, and your actions compare/contrast with the ungodly things that will soon be judged and destroyed?
4. How can we walk with God and be blameless in this generation?

Noah

Brad McKinnon

But between Heaven and us is an opening,
A porthole for a supplication.[1]

Focus Passage: Hebrews 11:7

One Main Thing: The righteousness that accompanies faith is a gift from God meant not just for those who might have been able to achieve remarkable records of obedience, but for those who have an imperfect, yet maturing respect for God. Folks who live out their faith from the heart find grace or favor in God's sight (Gen 6:8) and are thereby enabled by God to do extraordinary things.

Introduction

Extinction level events, followed up by post-apocalyptic chaos, is a typical Hollywood movie trope. These sorts of stories usually center around a male protagonist who goes to heroic lengths to keep his family safe. Even the subject of this chapter gets this treatment in the 2014 epic film *Noah* directed by Darren Aronofsky and featuring Russell Crowe as the title character.

---

[1] Adonis, "The New Noah," trans. by Shawkat M. Toorawa, *Poetry*, April 2007, 21–23.

In Hebrews 11, the Preacher[2] includes the same kind of conventions you might expect to see in a Hollywood blockbuster screenplay. Noah, facing seemingly insurmountable odds, constructs a large boat in the face of steep opposition and unforeseen challenges, and thus saves his family from certain doom from an impending flood.

Studies of Genesis 6–8 often assign an almost superhuman skill on the part of Noah to adhere to God's demands. After all, so the argument goes, Genesis 6:9 does describe Noah as "a righteous man [and] blameless." But looking closer at the broader context, Noah stands apart as blameless from a human population ("his generation") whose thoughts and imaginations are "only evil continually" (v. 5–9). That's not necessarily a very high standard of achievement. Even the most violent corners of our planet today couldn't be described as a continuous string of evil acts brought to life by evil inclinations. Your typical, imperfect average Joe or Jane would shine in an environment like the one described in Genesis 6. Thus, it shouldn't be terribly shocking that the first thing Noah does after leaving the ark is to plant a vineyard, get drunk, and help introduce some scandal into the family dynamic. The Preacher even seems to acknowledge this notion by avoiding any substantive discussion of Noah's personal character in Hebrews 11. While I wouldn't recommend completely overlooking the quality of Noah's character, there are

---

[2] Because the definitive identity of the author of the book of Hebrews is unknown to us and because the text doesn't have all the trappings of an ancient Greco-Roman letter, the text is sometimes considered more like a sermon or "word of exhortation" (Heb 13:22). Therefore, in this chapter, I'll refer to the writer as "the Preacher."

two interpretative keys highlighted by the Preacher that indicate he may be trying to do something a little different. These keys are an emphasis on Noah's faith coupled with a consideration of his inherited righteousness.

Noah is the third (after Abel and Enoch) in the first section of the list of faith's heroes in Hebrews 11.[3] Like the rest of the entries, the Preacher's discourse on Noah (11:7) begins with the introductory phrase "by faith." Both ancient and more contemporary writers have painted what I argue is an unrealistic portrait of Noah—a man of unassailable and pristine character who is able to obtain technical perfection in his obedience to God. The supposition is that this is why he found favor in the eyes of God to begin with. However, Noah wasn't perfect (in the absolute sense) after disembarking from the ark, because he wasn't perfect when boarding it. By definition, it's we imperfect people who need God's grace or favor. Noah found grace because he needed grace. But it was faith in such a gracious God that enabled Noah (and us) to accomplish marvelous things.

---

[3] I found the following resources helpful in preparing this material. I encourage you to consult these works for more detailed information about Hebrews 11, as well as Genesis 6–8. *The Epistle to the Hebrews* [Hermeneia Commentary] by Harold W. Attridge (Fortress, 1989); John Goldingay's *Genesis for Everyone* Part 1 (Westminster John Knox, 2010); *Hebrews* NTL by Luke Timothy Johnson (Westminster John Knox, 2006); *Hebrews* [Interpretation Commentary Series] by Thomas G. Long (Westminster John Knox, 1997); and N.T. Wright's *Hebrews for Everyone* (Westminster John Knox, 2004).

Interpretation

By faith. Faith is described in v. 1 as assurance and conviction of things either yet unknown or things unseen. Thus, faith serves as the foundation (ὑπόστασις; assurance) of a believer's life before God, and that foundation is constructed from evidence (ἔλεγχος; conviction) of God's unseen promises. For every man or woman of faith listed in Hebrews 11, belief is followed by an action of some sort or another. In Noah's case, by faith he built an ark (κιβωτὸν; box or chest) in order to save his family.

Seeing the unseen. The Preacher praises Noah for paying atten-tion to "events as yet unseen." While v. 3 describes faith as seeing what is invisible, in Noah's case, it wasn't as much about seeing what was invisible as it was seeing events yet to come. You see, faith isn't just conviction about the reality of invisible things, but it's also assurance of a future hope. As Thomas Long observes, "There was no evidence in the visible, sensory world to back up this word, so Noah had a choice to make: to trust what he saw around him with his own eyes or to trust God's word."[4] Noah chose to trust God even about things yet unseen; events that might have seemed unbelievable to him. Why did Noah respect the warning? Because of his reverence or piety, the Preacher says. This is the same term used to characterize Jesus in Hebrews 5:7. How did Jesus' piety manifest itself? Prayer, petition, and submission. I imagine something like this triad forming the basis for Noah's reverence as well.

---

[4] Thomas G. Long, *Hebrews*. Interpretation, (Louisville: Westminster John Knox, 1997), 117.

Condemned the world. Does the Preacher mean, as Luke Timothy Johnson puts it, that Noah's faith "was an implicit rebuke to the faithlessness and corruption of his contemporaries," or is this a reference to something akin to the tradition found in 2 Peter 2:5 ("Noah, a preacher of righteousness")?[5] In a setting like the one described in Genesis 6, I can imagine Noah both serving as a town crier of sorts—warning his neighbors of the coming disaster—while at the same time quietly rebuking them on the basis of his discernible allegiance to God.

Righteousness of faith. There's some question about the meaning of the phrase "righteousness of faith." Is it righteousness given by God because of faith alone and separate from works? Or is the idea that faith in God enabled Noah to do works of righteousness? My guess? It's not either/or, but both/and. Noah, as imperfect as he was, could do incredible things by God's grace, especially since his life was supported by a faith in God.

Application

There are several things we can learn about our own faith from this brief reference to Noah's in Hebrews 11. First, faith doesn't have to be superhuman to be worthy of emulation. Biblical faith is confidence in God, not in ourselves. Second, as one blogger has put it, faith is a learning-by-doing sort of process. When you do the things that faith does, faith gradually

---

[5] Luke Timothy Johnson, *Hebrews*. NTL (Louisville: Westminster John Knox, 2006), 285.

grows.[6] As the old cliché goes, "Fake it till you make it," or in C.S. Lewis's words, "faith is a habit that you have to train."[7] And third, faith often puts us at odds with the culture around us. Early Christians seemed to understand this, even if it posed challenges (like the pressures the recipients of the book of Hebrews were evidently facing). As Yale scholar Miroslav Volf reminds us:

> The early Christian communities were not major social players at all! They were not even among the cheering or booing spectators. Slandered, discriminated against, and even persecuted minorities, they were at most a bit of a thorn in society's flesh. Yet, notwithstanding their marginality, early Christian communities celebrated hope in God and proclaimed joyfully the resurrected Lord as they endeavored to walk in the footsteps of the crucified Messiah.[8]

Non-Western believers seem to grasp this concept out of necessity. It may be well past time to ask ourselves what faith would look like in a North American context that no longer privileges Christianity.

---

[6] Alan Brahm, "Helping Our Unbelief," The Waking Dreamer (blog), August 13, 2010, http://thewakingdreamer.blogspot.com/2010/08/helping-our-unbelief-heb.html.

[7] C.S. Lewis, *Mere Christianity* (New York: Scribner, 1952), 109.

[8] Miroslav Volf, *A Public Faith: How Followers of Christ Should Serve the Common Good* (Grand Rapids: Brazos, 2011), 78.

Conclusion

There's an old saying that "Perfect is the enemy of good." Maybe in our pursuit of righteous perfection personified in Noah, we've missed the good. That as men and women of faith (as imperfect as we are), we are marked as God's people so that even under unimaginable worst-case scenarios (personal, familial, communal, or global), God always provides an opening for reconciliation. In Noah's case, when "the windows of the heavens were opened," it brought destruction, but it also brought reconciliation. Today, God has opened "a porthole for a supplication" between heaven and earth. Through faith and the righteousness that comes with it, this opening brings renewal.

Discussion

1. How does viewing Noah as a profoundly ordinary man help us focus on the greatness of God?
2. In what ways has your faith enabled you to do significant things by the grace of God? Can you name an example or two?
3. How does "seeing things (yet) unseen" speak to our own faith today as we eagerly wait for the coming of the Lord?
4. The world faces many challenges today. Challenges that aren't necessarily unique or unprecedented, but unnerving, nonetheless. Natural disasters. Political volatility. Economic uncertainty. Deadly violence. International health crises. How do times like these provide opportunities to show greater trust in God, as well as opportunities to reconcile not just with God, but with the world around us?

Abraham

Michael Jackson

Focus Passage: Hebrews 11:8

One Main Thing: Abraham provides an example of someone who was willing to give up something significant in the belief that he would gain something more important by following God's will, compelling us to ask ourselves, "What holds me back?"

Introduction

I've never been very good at giving things up. If you come to my house, that will be readily apparent. We have a guest bedroom that is filled with stuff that I promised I would go through when we moved (a year ago). If you look in the closet in that same room, you will find my baseball cards from when I was a kid. It drives some people crazy, but I even hang on to the boxes that my electronics come in.

I learned the hard way that I "come by it honest," as we say here in the South. When my dad died and my mom was diagnosed with frontotemporal dementia, my brothers and I were tasked with going through all of the stuff. It was overwhelming to say the least. You really get to know someone when you are shredding their bank statements from 1962.

Thus far, all I've talked about is stuff. I have a hard time giving up stuff, but an even harder time giving up things like family and my home.

When Dad died, there were times where I felt so sad and lonely even when I was completely surrounded by love and support. And when Mom was diagnosed and soon after lost her ability to speak, I felt like all of my stories from my entire life, and all the things I'd ever want to know about the past, went with her. I still have moments where I want to call and talk with them and share some of the simple or silly things that families know and share with one another. I wasn't ready to give them up.

I, like a lot of other people, also do as much as I can to protect my property and my home. One of my first purchases after moving was a security system with security cameras. I have insurance on my home to ensure that if anything happens to it, it can be replaced on the same property. I can walk my dog even when I am half asleep because I know exactly how many paces to move in the dark to get to the door and get him outside at night.

Do you ever go out of town for a couple of days of sleeping at a hotel, and then you get to lay on your bed at home for the first time in a while? How does that feel? Is there anything scientifically different from your bed at home and the ones in the hotel? What makes it so special? It is special because it is home.

And home is made up of all of these things we've just talked about, including stuff, but more especially the people and the place where we dwell.

So, what if I were asked to give those things up for God? What if God needed me or asked me to sacrifice these things in service to Him?

I must admit to you today that I'm not sure what I'd do. And that's just the kind of sentiment that the biblical writers acknowledge in the stories we are going to examine today of the great patriarch Abraham.

Going Deeper

In Hebrews 11, as we continue our series on the faith that we should emulate, our focus in this lesson will be verses 8–10 and 13–19.

And by way of reminder, the context of Hebrews 11 is in the wake of the Hebrew writer's admonition to his audience in Hebrews 10 that they should not shrink back and lose their endurance (Heb 10:36). The list and encouragement of Hebrews 11 and 12 is intentional—it is designed for us as Christians to look over and be inspired. This is not just a cute story—the stakes are real, and they are high. If we do not endure, the Hebrew writer makes it clear that we will not receive the promises.

We are encouraged to have faith like Abraham in order to help us endure. The simple question of our lesson is, "Do I have faith like Abraham?"

I would like for us to pursue this question by framing our Abraham stories in Hebrews 11 the way R.W.L. Moberly so eloquently frames the story (building off of Nahum Sarna's JPS Commentary on Genesis), when he says:

> "At the beginning, Abraham is commanded to relinquish his past, And at the end, Abraham is commanded to relinquish his future." [1]

---

[1] Moberly, R. W. L., *The Theology of the Book of Genesis*, (New York: Cambridge University Press, 2009), 186.

A Faith that Gives Up the Past

The first story that we encounter in Hebrews 11 that references Abraham's life is in verses 8–10, as the Hebrew writer reminds us of Abraham's faith when he was still Abram, in Genesis 12.

The calling of Abraham is perhaps one of the most significant events in biblical history, and hopefully it is a story that everyone has learned or heard from childhood. But even if not, the Hebrew writer provides a great synopsis in verse 8 of that faith that has been renowned for thousands of years—the faith of Abram to leave his father's house and go wherever God told him to go.

The Hebrew writer fills us in on an important detail for his purposes, in that he tells us that "Abram did not know where he was going." In this detail, he is following the narrative that we read in Genesis, in that Abram doesn't find out his new home until after he arrives there (verses 6–7). This is important in Hebrews, as it emphasizes the definition of faith in Hebrews 11:1 as the "conviction of things not seen." Abraham's willingness to trust God even in the unknown is the kind of faith we should have.

All of this is framed in an act of leaving some significant things behind. In the story in Genesis (12:1), Abram is told to go forth from his country, his relatives, and his father's house. Notice the funnel of the narrative there, how it starts big and then gets down to the very specific—country, relatives, father's house. God's calling of Abram required big time faith. He had to give up that which he knew, on faith, in order to work towards that which he could not yet see.

It might be argued that by virtue of following Jesus, we have been called to just as radical a faith as Abraham, although it takes a different shape under the new covenant—Jesus says that we must have a faith that will cause us to deny even ourselves. Listen to these words of Jesus:

> [24]If anyone wishes to come after Me, he must deny himself, and take up his cross and follow Me. [25]For whoever wishes to save his life will lose it; but whoever loses his life for My sake will find it. [26]For what will it profit a man if he gains the whole world and forfeits his soul? Or what will a man give in exchange for his soul? (Matt 16:24-26 NASB)

I believe we see in Abraham an example of someone who was willing to give up something significant on the faith that he would gain something more important by following God's will.

So, the question comes to you and me: Do we have that kind of faith? What do I struggle to let go of? What can't I seem to leave behind?

Until we answer those questions, we will be like the rich young ruler in chapter 10 of Mark's gospel, who struggled with Jesus' intense request of faith.

The Hebrew writer says that as a result of his faith, Abraham was always a sojourner, even in the promised land. And in verses 13-16, he is clear to point out that if Abram thought about the country which he came out of, he would have had time to return there, but instead, he pressed on in faith. The point the writer is trying to make is that Abraham didn't dwell on his previous home, and therefore he must have had in mind a greater homeland—a heavenly one.

So again, I ask you, what holds you back? What in your past have you struggled to give up in faith that God will have something better in store for you, that may not even be in this life?

A Faith that Gives Up the Future to God

The other story that the Hebrew writer reminds us of is a difficult one from the Genesis account of Abraham's life. The connection that is made here between Genesis 12 and Genesis 22 is not only obvious in Hebrews, but has long been recognized by Jewish commentators to be connected by similar language in the opening of both stories ("Go forth"), and according to Sarna, that language does not occur again in the Old Testament.

The story of Abraham's willingness to offer his son Isaac, with simple faith because God asks him to, is shocking to the modern mind. The history of interpretation on this story is fascinating. Throughout history the story has been generally received positively, with Abraham as a model of faith. And that is certainly the way the Hebrew writer sees the story.

But Moberly also shares with us many accounts where the story is received negatively, and for many different reasons. Even Immanuel Kant, the noted philosopher, comments on the story that Abraham should have spoken back to God and said, "I'm not sure you are really God." That sentiment has continued through many interpreters who see in the story a symbol of child abuse and child sacrifice.

Soren Kierkegaard even has spoken of something called the "Nightmare Scenario," where someone might hear of this story and then go home and sacrifice their child to God. Unfortunately, this happened in 1990 in California.

So, we must first address that using Genesis 22 to support a "blind faith" that encourages child abuse or sacrifice is a wrong use of Genesis 22. You must notice that Hebrews 11 doesn't even im-agine a sense in which this kind of interpretation could take place. And when we read Scripture holistically, we see clearly that God does not accept child sacrifice:

> They have built the high places of Topheth, which is in the valley of the son of Hinnom, to burn their sons and their daughters in the fire, which I did not command, and it did not come into My mind (Jer 7:31 NASB).

We should also point out that the story is placed in a very specific context. In Genesis, against all odds, Sarah finally gives birth to Isaac in chapter 21. We see now that the promise, which was so long in the making, now finally rests with Isaac. This is indicated in the story itself, where Isaac is called Abraham's "only" son (22:2), which he wasn't biologically, but he was in terms of the promise (it is used as a meaning of value).

Finally, we are told from the very outset that God "tested" Abraham. Don't underestimate the clue that this gives us to the story. Sarna says at this point, when we read this, it allows us to relax, and to know that this story isn't about Isaac and what is going to happen to him. This story is about Abraham!

And what do we learn about Abraham's faith from the story? In Genesis 22:12, the angel of the LORD says, "now I know that you fear God." So, was it that God didn't know something? Is his omniscience in question?

I don't think so. I think this mixes up the entire point of the story. Why does God test Abraham? To learn some new information about whether or not he would pass the test? I don't think so. This is a test of experience and not a test of knowledge. God tests Abraham to understand where he is in his relationship with God, and whether or not he fully believes and is willing to give himself over to that belief through ultimate trust. As Moberly puts it, when Abraham is depicted as one who fears God, the divine pronouncement of "now I know" ... indicates that the deepened relationship is in some way an intrinsic concern of God...[2]

I think this is reflected in the Hebrew writer's statement in Hebrews 11:19, where he says that Abraham trusted God so much that he believed that God would raise Isaac up from the dead to fulfill the promise. What faith! And James would frame Abraham's faith in the form of relationship with God when he says in James 2:23 that Abraham was "called the friend of God."

Abraham was willing to place his entire future promise, the one he left his entire family to pursue, in the hands of God (believing that God would take care of him)!

Where have you placed your future? Do you place your future in the hands of money, or success, or security? Or have you placed it in the hands of God?

When God says about you, "now I know that you _____," what goes in that blank? What does God know about you?

---

[2] Moberly, R. W. L., *The Bible, Theology, and Faith: A Study of Abraham and Jesus*, (New York: Cambridge University Press, 2000), 107.

Discussion Questions

1. How is Abraham's faith, as described in Hebrews 11, related to the "definition of faith" in Hebrews 11:1?
2. What do you think it means to "give up the past" for God? What does it look like when someone trusts God in this way?
3. What do you think it means to "give up the future" to God? What does it look like when someone trusts God in this way?
4. What do you believe was the purpose of God's testing of Abraham in Genesis 22? How does this relate to Abraham's faith?
5. What one thing can you do today to be more like Abraham in your faith?

Sarah

Justin Guin

Focus Passage: Hebrews 11:11
One Main Thing: Sarah provides a valuable example of faith that overcomes impatience and doubt.

Introduction

One of the great challenges of life is walking by faith and not by sight (cf. 2 Cor 5:7; Matt 7:13–14). We live in an age of scientific deduction which often leaves little room for spiritual realities. If we cannot see, touch, smell, or taste it then it does not exist. This has led our world to become increasingly secular. Living by faith requires us to swim against the current of popular culture.

A study of scripture proves this struggle is not new. While the incidentals may be different, people of faith have always overcome obstacles which sought to undermine their convictions. In Hebrews 11, the examples of those who lived by faith surround us with a "great cloud of witnesses" cheering us on in our own sojourn of faith (Heb 12:1–2). One such example is Sarah. She is only mentioned in Hebrews 11:11, and when you consider her example against the historical record of Genesis, you see the challenges she overcame. She endured moments of doubt, frustration, anger, and hopelessness. All these emotions are relatable to every person. Testing can cause us to act in self-interest and desperation. Despite it all, she lived by faith. Sarah's example teaches us that living by faith overcomes obstacles through an enduring trust in the surety of God word.

The story of Abraham's family begins in Hebrews 11:8 and continues through 11:22. The theme of this section is faith's focus on God's promise. Abraham, Sarah, Isaac, Jacob, and Joseph all lived by faith because they believed God is faithful to his promises. God promised to bless all nations through Abraham's seed (Gen 12:1–3). This is no doubt an enigma to a couple who had been barren well into old age. This promise provides the foundation of everything they do, and each is commended for responding to God in submission and obedience.

In Hebrews 11:11, Sarah's faith is commended: "By faith Sarah herself received power to conceive, even when she was past the age, since she considered him faithful who had promised" (ESV). When you consider Sarah's choices in Genesis 12–21, this statement can seem puzzling. When it came to fulfilling God's promise of a great nation through Abraham's seed, she responded in doubt and even tried to take matters into her own hands. We are reminded that faithfulness does not demand perfection. Instead, it requires an enduring trust in God. He will provide. A look at Genesis will help us understand both Sarah's faith and struggles.

Going Deeper

In Genesis 12–21, Sarah is mentioned three times in relation to providing Abraham a son. The first is found in Genesis 16 where she offers her servant, Hagar, as her surrogate. No doubt the struggle of infertility took its toll on Abraham's wife, but she had a solution. She told him, "The Lord has prevented me from bearing children. Go in to my servant; it may be that I shall obtain children by her" (16:2). During this time, infertility was viewed as a curse from God. In the ancient world, women obtained honor through marriage and childbearing. Surrogacy was attested for remedying childlessness. Sarah's barrenness brought dishonor to her husband and meant she would not be the one to fulfill the God-given promise to make of him a great nation. So, offering Hagar as a replacement meant she could bring honor to the patriarch and leader of the family as Hagar had no legal claim to the child. Children born to her belonged to Sarah.[1] This situation quickly turned ugly. In 16:5, Sarah complained to Abraham that her servant looked at her with contempt. With Abraham's permission she dismissed Hagar to the wilderness. Ishmael would be blessed, but he was not the promised offspring of Abraham.

The next scene is found in Genesis 17–18. In these chapters, God affirmed for a third time his covenant with Abraham and Sarah. In Genesis 17:16, the Lord promised, "I will bless her and moreover, I will give you a son by her. I will bless her, and she shall become nations; and kings of peoples." For the first time, the promise to Abraham is now extended directly to his wife. The thought of these two bearing children in their old age seemed preposterous. Note how Abraham responded, "Then Abraham fell on his face and laughed and said to himself, 'Shall a child be born to a man who is a hundred years old? Shall Sarah, who is ninety years

---

[1] John Walton, Victor H. Matthews, and Mark W. Chavalas, *The IVP Bible Background Commentary: Old Testament*, Electronic Ed. (Downers Grove: InterVarsity Press, 2000), n.p.; Kenneth A. Mathews, *Genesis 11:27-50:26* NAC 1B (Nashville: Broadman and Holman, 2005), 177.

old, bear a child?'" (17:17). The answer is simply "yes." God confirmed the promise in v. 18.

In the next chapter, the Lord appeared again to Abraham (18:1). Three travelers were invited by him to stay in his home and were shown great hospitality. Abraham provided for them food and lodging, and they revealed his promised son would be born about a year later. The text clearly ruled out Sarah's ability to conceive a child. She was advanced in years and past the age of childbearing. The only way this could happen was through the Lord's intervention. Overhearing their conversation, Sarah responded in the same manner as Abraham in Genesis 17:17. Laughing to herself she said, "After I am worn out, and my lord is old, shall I have pleasure?" Such an attitude doubted the Lord's promise to which the men responded, "Is anything too hard for the Lord?" When confronted by the men about laughing, she denied it because she was afraid (18:15). The way the men miraculously knew her thoughts gave credibility to their promise of a coming child.[2]

The final scene occurs in Genesis 21. God is faithful, and the fulfillment of his promise brought hope to a hopeless couple. The thought of Sarah bearing a child seemed absurd even when heavenly messengers from the Lord predicted it just a year prior. Genesis 21:1 says the Lord "visited" the them. When the Lord visited someone in Old Testament it refers to divine intervention. God miraculously enabled Sarah to conceive and bear a son, and his birth was at the "appointed time" (HCSB). It was all according to God's timing and providence. Abraham

---

[2] Matthews, 219.

named him Isaac, which means "he laughs." This was a fitting name since the promise of his birth brought both of his parents to laughter. Furthermore, taking away her barrenness brought joy to Sarah and she exclaimed, "God has made laughter for me; everyone who hears will laugh over me" (v. 6). God kept his promise. Through the Lord, Abraham and Sarah became a great nation.

Application

After working through the historical account in Genesis, it seems a bit strange to commend Sarah for her faith. Just the opposite seemed to be true. She doubted, laughed, and even tried to secure the outcome by acting outside of God's providential plan. Her example reveals the struggle of faithfulness. Note a few obstacles that Sarah overcame in her journey of faith.

First, Sarah overcame the problem of impatience. God's initial promise to Abraham occurred twenty-five years before Isaac's birth. Moreover, Sarah waited 90 years to give birth to a child. Our own experiences remind us how impatience can exhaust our trust. Patience only comes in two ways—waiting and suffering. Neither is pleasant, and Sarah experienced both.

When we're waiting on the Lord, impatience can undermine our faith and motivate us to act irrationally and rashly. First, we act irrationally. We quickly forget the many acts of God's faithfulness in the past. The Lord had been faithful to Sarah and her family. Why would this change now? Also, acting irrationally causes us to do things we normally would not do. Sarah trying to take matters into her own hands, used Hagar as a surrogate. This was not God's plan and it was doomed for failure. In fact, it exacerbated the problem, causing tension and bitterness between the two women (cf. Gen 21:8ff). Sarah's example reminds us that an enduring faith requires patience. The term translated "patience" in the New Testament refers to the capacity to bear up under trials.

    1. In Galatians 5:23, we're told it is the fruit of the Spirit. How do we know we are living by the Spirit's instruction? We have patience.

    2. In Colossians 3:12, we are commanded to "put on" several characteristics which are opposed to sinful living. One of those is patience.

    3. In Hebrews 6:12, patience and faith keep us from becoming, "sluggish" instead living with zeal and assurance.

A second obstacle that Sarah overcame was the detriment of doubt. As noted, the text is clear that Sarah could not naturally have children. In Hebrews 11:11, Sarah is described as one who was "past age." In the next verse, Abraham is described as one who was "as good as dead" when it came to producing children. So, it is understandable for both to respond with laughter and unbelief with the Lord told them Sarah would give birth to a son. They fell prey to Satan's oldest scheme, namely tempting us to doubt the truthfulness of God's word. In the Garden, when he tempted Adam and Eve he led with, "Did God actually say…" (Gen. 3:1). In the case of Abraham and Sarah, what had God said? He reaffirmed his covenant with Abraham several times, reminding him he would father a great nation, Sarah would give birth to the child, and it would be the Lord's doing. But they, relying solely on human experience, doubted God's promise.

If we are going to live by faith, we must overcome the detriment of doubt. Doubt undermines our trust in the Lord and is a characteristic of a weak faith. The Lord rebuked Peter in Matthew 14:31, "O you of little faith, why did you doubt?" What can we do to strengthen our faith against this scheme of Satan? First, we must draw near to God in full assurance of faith. In Hebrews, we find this exhortation two times (Heb 6:11; 10:22). The word "full assurance" means to be completely certain of the truth of something.[3] Faith is based on the unchangeable nature of God and the surety of his word (Heb 6:16–17). Second, we must focus on the truth and not become distracted by Satan's deceptive tactics. We must keep in mind, "What did God *actually* say?" Such flips Satan's attempt on its end. He desires nothing more than for us to forget what God has told us.

Conclusion

In the end, Sarah considered the Lord to be faithful to his promise. Her example teaches us that living by faith overcomes obstacles through an enduring trust in the surety of God's word. Through the circumstances, Satan tried to undermine her faith. But an enduring faith focuses on God and his promise. Let that be the lesson we learn from this great matriarch of the faith.

---

[3] Eugene A. Nida and Johannes P. Louw, *Greek-English Lexicon Based on Semantic Domains*, (New York: American Bible Society, 1989), 1:370.

Discussion Questions

1. Considering the historical account of Genesis, why might it seem odd to commend Sarah for her faith? What does this teach us about living by faith?
2. Why is it tempting to take matters in our own hands like Sarah? What consequences did she reap later for this decision?
3. How does impatience weaken our faith? Why might it be intimidating to pray for faith?
4. How did Satan work to get Sarah to doubt the promise of God? What does doubt do to our faith, and how can we work throughout doubts to become stronger?

Joseph
Nathan Daily

Focus Passages: Hebrews 11:22 and Genesis 50:25

One Main Thing: In Hebrews, faith is not simply equated with belief but consists of past, present, and future orientations of remembrance, trust, and hope.

Introduction

> *"I will honour Christmas in my heart, and try to keep it all the year. I will live in the Past, the Present, and the Future. The Spirits of all Three shall strive within me. I will not shut out the lessons that they teach…"*
>
> *Holding up his hands in a last prayer to have his fate reversed, he saw an alteration in the Phantom's hood and dress. It shrunk, collapsed, and dwindled down into a bedpost.*
>
> *Yes! And the bedpost was his own. The bed was his own, the room was his own. Best and happiest of all, the Time before him was his own, to make amends in!*
>
> *"I will live in the Past, the Present, and the Future!" Scrooge repeated, as he scrambled out of bed.*[1]

---

[1] Charles Dickens, *A Christmas Carol. In Prose. Being a Ghost Story of Christmas* (London: Chapman & Hall, 1843; repr. Modern Library; New York: Random House, 1995), 98–99.

A human life is not lived "in the moment" but is a complex interaction between the past, present, and future. Dickens's portrayal of Scrooge's transformation from self-interest toward introspection epitomized through Scrooge's language upon awakening offers a gorgeous reminder that fullness and meaning derive from living outside the present and the self. Striving beyond the moment, into the past and future, provides impetus for seeking meaning beyond isolation and individualism and is a beginning point for a wholistic approach to being human.

The book of Hebrews also offers past, present, and future as a key for articulating a wholistic approach to life. In this case, the focus is faith. By defining faith and providing examples of lives from Scripture, Hebrews encourages a life of faith that extends beyond any simplistic reductionism and, rather, expects action and even endurance. Here, our focus is on Hebrews 11's concluding example from the book of Genesis, Joseph. The narratives of Jacob's sons in Genesis 37–50 provide several opportunities for finding examples of faith in the life of Joseph. At the hands of his own family, Joseph is ridiculed, nearly murdered, and sold into slavery. Living in a foreign country he is falsely accused, sent to prison, and forgotten by those he helps. In time, he becomes known as a dream interpreter, rises to second in command of Egypt, and even saves the world from famine. Near the end of this story of suffering, Joseph is finally reunited with his family. Even this far too simple outline provides much fodder for presenting a faithful Joseph, but Hebrews uses none of this. Rather, Hebrews 11:22 offers a restatement of one cryptic line from the end of Joseph's life as the demonstration that Joseph lived by faith.

Going Deeper

As we engage Hebrews' comment on the faith of Joseph,[2] first, we should remind ourselves of the guiding definition of faith the book provides in 11:1-3: "Now faith is the assurance of things hoped for, the conviction of things not seen.... By faith we understand that the ages were prepared by the word of God..." Even though we could discuss the logistics of this definition for quite some time, I simply want us to notice the past, present, and future orientation inherent in the definition. Faith is much more than "belief in God."[3] According to Hebrews, the past ("the ages were prepared by the word of God"), the present ("faith is"), and the future ("hope") operate together to present faith as trust (assurance, conviction, understanding) that what is either seen or unseen, the entirety of the reality created and ordered by God, was, is, and will be sourced in God. Faith is trust that all visible is not self-sufficient but derives from invisible (God).[4] Trust, or conviction, in the past and future actions of the Creator sustains a disposition of confidence in the present. This we call faith.

Of all the possibilities for illustrations that could be mined from the narratives of the life of Joseph, Hebrews 11:22 chooses Joseph's

---

[2] This reading of Hebrews is highly dependent on Luke Timothy Johnson, *Hebrews: A Commentary* NTL (Louisville: Westminster John Knox, 2006), 274-97. See also, Thomas G. Long, *Hebrews* [Interpretation] (Louisville: Westminster John Knox, 1997), 112-121; N. T. Wright, *Hebrews for Everyone* (Louisville: Westminster John Knox, 2003), 126-39; Fred B. Craddock, NIB 12:1-174.

[3] Rowan Williams, *Tokens of Trust: An Introduction to Christian Belief* (Louisville: Westminster John Knox, 2007), 3-30.

[4] Johnson, *Hebrews*, 280.

statement in Genesis 50:25, "When God comes to you, you shall carry up my bones from here," as the opportunity for a lesson on faith from Joseph's life: "By faith, as he was coming to an end, Joseph remembered the exodus of the children of Israel and gave commands concerning his bones."[5] What, at first, seems an obscure choice, upon reflection, becomes an intriguing model of Hebrews' definition of faith. As Joseph's life "comes to an end," he "remembers" the Exodus which, of course, has not yet happened. Therefore, remembering the Exodus must be equivalent to re-membering God's promise of the Exodus to Abraham in Genesis 15:13–15. Even after all the suffering throughout his life, Joseph, at the end of his life, so confidently trusts, or has faith, in the promise of the still distant future that he provides instructions for his own remains. Joseph's speaking and acting, retelling a promise from the time of Abraham and requesting his bones be brought out of Egypt in a time to come, reflect Hebrews' definition of the life of faith. Through Joseph's expression of certainty about the invisible within his visible present reality, Hebrews offers a succinct picture of a life lived in faith / trust / certainty in the present because of faith / trust / assurance in the past and faith / trust / hope for the future.

Application

Reading Hebrews helps us read the Hebrew Scriptures in new ways, ways we would not have imagined on our own. Following the well-known but profound Dickensian rubric

---

[5] Translation of Johnson, *Hebrews*, 287.

provided in Scrooge's exclamation, "I will live in the Past, the Present, and the Future!" coupled with Hebrews' own definition of faith, we will consider the broader Joseph narrative of Genesis in dialogue with Hebrews' presentation of Joseph to articulate avenues for Christian practice.

As a declaration of living by faith, "I live in the Past" serves as a posture of certainty connecting the Christian to all the people of God and the ancient promises of God. Hebrews finds this faith in Joseph as Joseph "remembers" God's ancient promise to Abraham. Genesis 37–50[6] explicitly states that God is "with" Joseph and "blesses" him (Gen 39), yet, for readers, the substance of God's presence appears much less explicitly with Joseph than earlier in Genesis with Abraham and Sarah as well as later with the plague narratives in Exodus or the wilderness wanderings of Israel in Numbers. As he lives much of his life as an object of hatred, a slave, a prisoner, and displaced in a foreign land, Joseph's own words appeal to a certainty: God is present. Upon revealing himself to his brothers, Joseph says, "God sent me here before you to preserve life" (45:5) and to "preserve a remnant" (45:7). Joseph even goes as far as to say, "it was not you who sent me here, but God" (45:8). In response to the fear if his brothers upon

---

[6] On the theology of Genesis 37–50 see, Gary A. Anderson, *Christian Doctrine and the Old Testament: Theology in the Service of Biblical Exegesis* (Grand Rapids: Baker Academic, 2017), 75–94; R. W. L. Moberly, *The Theology of the Book of Genesis,* Old Testament Theology (Cambridge: Cambridge University Press, 2009), 225–46; Jon D. Levenson, *The Death and Resurrection of the Beloved Son: The Transformation of Child Sacrifice in Judaism and Christianity* (New Haven: Yale, 1993), 143–172.

the death of their father, Joseph says, "Even though you intended to do harm to me, God intended it for good, in order to preserve a numerous people, as he is doing today" (50:20). And nearing death, Joseph somberly prophesies "I am about to die; but God will surely visit you and bring you up out of this land to the land that he swore to Abraham, Isaac, and Jacob" (50:24). Joseph's certainty of God's involvement receives coherence through the larger Genesis narrative, specifically God's promise of children, great nation, blessing, and land to the ancestors (Gen 12:1–3). Joseph repeats the themes of the promise to his great-grandparents, Abraham and Sarah, because he lives by faith, a certain trust of God gained from the past.

As a declaration of living by faith, "I live in the Present" constructs a moment of assurance, in dialogue with the past and future, providing the Christian an expression of peace in the midst of difficulty. Hebrews finds this faith in Joseph when positioning Joseph's decision near the moment of his death in relation to God's promise, both past (remembering promise and future (land of promise. Similar examples of Joseph's present decisions being influenced by past and future are plentiful in Genesis 37–50. Joseph's rejection of the proposition by Potiphar's wife is, in his words, "a sin against God" (39:9). This language exposes a past engagement with and a future expectation of relationship with God on the part of Joseph. Joseph's rise in Potiphar's house and in Pharaoh's kingdom as well as his extensive plan to save the world from famine (41:33–36) are certainly related to his wise choices in the present, but, once again, according to Joseph, all these are the doings of God ("Do not interpretations belong to God," 40:8; "It is not I, God will give Pharaoh a favorable answer," 41:16; "God has revealed to Pharaoh what he is about to do," 41:25; "God has made me lord of all Egypt," 45:9; "Am I in the place of God," 50:19; "God intended it for good," 50:20). The reuniting of the brothers in Egypt is a particularly telling indicator for Joseph's life of faith. "Living in the present" might offer a temptation to enact the old proverb "revenge is a dish best served cold" upon the sight of these brothers after years of separation and rising to a position of power. The brothers certainly expect such (42:28; 50:15). Though Joseph's interactions with his brothers are, to say the least, complex, his ultimate reaction to their presence betrays not a reaction to the present situation but fear of God (42:18), a sense of familial fidelity (50:17), and posture of forgiveness that leaves vengeance to God (50:19; cf. Deut 32:35; Heb 10:30). Is Joseph among the wise? Probably (41:39). Is Joseph among the faithful? Joseph's "in the moment" decisions appear to be grounded in much beyond the present tense, what Hebrews quantifies as "by faith."

As a declaration of living by faith, "I live in the Future" imports hope and confidence into the present, a trust in the invisible and in the movement from death to life. Hebrews finds this faith in Joseph amid his declaration to move his bones to the land promised by God. For Joseph, death is not the end. The fulfillment of all the promises of God is the only end. In Genesis, Joseph's life displays striking movement from death to life. Joseph's path from death to life begins as he is stripped of his coat and thrown into a pit (37:20–23) and ultimately "goes down" to Egypt (39:1). Elsewhere, the pit is a synonym for Sheol, the place of the dead, as well as a metaphor for a dire situation of distress (Isa 14:15; 38:18; Ps 28:1; 30:3; 88:4).

In fact, throughout the narrative, Joseph is understood as dead (37:35; 42:38; 44:20; cf. 46:30). Yet, directly paralleling earlier moments in the story, after a time in Egypt, Joseph is raised up from a different pit and given new clothing (40:15; 41:14) as the first step of his rising in power (44:18; 45:8) toward the fulfillment of his original dreams (37:10; 44:30–33; 50:18). Intertwining this theme with Joseph's own language of God's involvement in the narrative (45:9; 50:20; etc.), Joseph's movement from suffering / abandonment / death toward life / reconciliation / resurrection enhances the message of living in the future where trust extends any present situation, positive or negative, into hope and confidence. Joseph's life ends living in the future and citing the past with a hope that his people will rise up even more: "I am about to die; but God will *visit* you, and *bring you up* out of this land to the land that he swore to Abraham, to Isaac, and to Jacob" (50:24). Joseph's life is not complete with his death. His bones must move because there is a future to the story, and, if God made a promise in the past, Joseph expects to be part of that promise in the future, a future orientation that Hebrew labels, by faith.

Conclusion

Hebrews claims that Christians "have tasted the goodness of the word of God and the powers of the age to come" (6:4). That is, we have tasted (already) the future age (that which is not-yet). A life lived in the past, present, and future is central to Christian self-understanding and practice. If our present disposition is an endeavor to retain connection with God's past promises (Gen 12) and to maintain confidence in that future tasted through Jesus' resurrection (1 Cor 10:11; 2 Cor 5:17; Rom 6), then like Joseph, engagement in the present becomes a matter of certainty, assurance, and hope, so it goes by faith.

Discussion

1. What is the definition of faith in Hebrews 11:1–3? How does this definition help you explain the meaning of faith?
2. Identify some reasons Hebrews might have chosen Genesis 50:25 to depict the faith of Joseph. If you were to pick one verse or text from Genesis to show Joseph lived by faith, what would you choose? Why?
3. How did Joseph, by faith, live in the past, the present, and the future? How do the past, present, and future impact the life of faith for you, your family, and your worshipping community?
4. Is there a time where your experiences from the past or your hope for the future impacted a decision you made in the present?
5. Why does Joseph give instructions about his bones? How can we read these instructions as a theological statement?
6. How does the promise to Abraham help us live in the past? Are there other Old Testament texts that would offer a similar foundation for us?
7. How does the resurrection of Jesus help us live in the present and the future? What other biblical texts help us to think about the present in light of the future?
8. What promises of God give you hope?

Moses

C. Wayne Kilpatrick

Focus Passage: Exodus 33:12-19; 34:6

One Main Thing: God chose Moses and prepared him through his life experiences for roles in leadership, intercession for others, and as a lawgiver. Moses demonstrated his faith in God by his actions.

Introduction

Moses is mentioned by name 784 times in the Bible. Only David (968 times) and Jesus (940 times) were mentioned in more verses than Moses. One can see the great importance God placed upon Moses in his word. God, through his providential workings, protected Moses from birth to the grave. Only Moses was privileged to see God's glory in its near fullness (Exod 33:17-23). Neither Abraham nor David was given that privilege. Moses' strong faith in God produced at least four qualities of Moses.

When we look upon Moses as an ordinary man, we still see God's hand upon him, because of his strong active faith. He was born during turbulent times, into the house of Levi, at a time when "there arose up a new king over Egypt, which knew not Joseph (Exod 1:8). This king or pharaoh enslaved the children of Israel and put harsh tasks upon them. Eventually, he ordered the midwives to kill all male Hebrew babies at birth (Exod 1:22). Moses' parents through faith saw that he was no ordinary child and risked everything to preserve him (Heb 11:23). God, through his providence, caused Moses to be placed in the bulrushes for protection, and it was God's providence that brought a sympathetic-hearted daughter of pharaoh to the riverbank, who took Moses home with her to raise as her own (Exod 2:5–10; Heb 11:23). This again was God's providence which placed Moses in the household of the very man who was seeking his life. This act of God positioned Moses so he could be educated by the best educators in Egypt (Acts 7:22). "And Moses was learned in all the wisdom of the Egyptians and was mighty in words and in deeds."

When Moses reached manhood, he was drawn to his biological family—the Hebrews. "And it came to pass in those days, when Moses was grown, that he went out unto his brethren, and looked on their burdens: and he spied an Egyptian smiting a Hebrew, one of his brethren. And he looked this way and that way, and when he saw that there was no man, he slew the Egyptian, and hid him in the sand (Exod 2:11–12). At this point Moses' patriotism was revealed. He killed to defend his people. Moses chose his afflicted people over all of Egypt's wealth and comfort. The Hebrew writer says the forsaking all Egypt had to offer him was done through faith (Heb 11:24–25):"By faith Moses, when he was come to years, refused to be called the son of Pharaoh's daughter; Choosing rather to suffer affliction with the people of God, than to enjoy the pleas-ures of sin for a season." The writer of Hebrews also says that Moses esteemed the reproach of Christ greater than all of Egypt's riches "for he had respect unto the recompense of the reward" (Heb 11:26). Pharaoh sought Moses intending to kill him, forcing him to go into hiding in Midian. In so doing, Moses became a "criminal on the run." This was all done in faith, and God re-sponded by protecting him.

Going Deeper

The slaying of the Egyptian was not the only time Moses defended his people. After God chose Moses to lead his people out of Egypt to the Promised land, he had to openly plead to God on their behalf. In Exodus 32:7-14, the children of Israel worshipped the golden calf while Moses was on the mountain with God, receiving the "Ten Commandments." God decided to destroy unfaithful Israel. "Now therefore let me alone, that my wrath may wax hot against them, and that I may consume them: and I will make of thee a great nation. And Moses besought the LORD his God, and said, LORD, why doth thy wrath wax hot against thy people, which thou hast brought forth out of the land of Egypt with great power, and with a mighty hand?" (Exod 32:10-11) Moses interceded on behalf of Israel (Exod 32: 12-13). Out of being a fugitive Moses became a leader of God's people; but more than a leader he became an intercessor on behalf of God's people when he basically threw himself between God and fallen Israel. This interceding on behalf of Israel continued through (Exod 32:30-34). Moses pled with the point that he finally said: "Yet now, if thou wilt forgive their sin; and if not, blot me, I pray thee, out of thy book which thou hast written" (Exod 32:32). God yields to Moses' request and only punishes the guilty.

In Numbers 14 God was once again angered and ready to destroy all the people, and Moses interceded on their behalf. On this occasion the people rebelled against Moses' and Aaron's leadership and God intervened. Once again, he was ready to destroy the entire nation of people. On three occasions Moses has shown himself to be a good intercessor, as well as a good leader.

Moses also was designated as a law giver on Mt. Sinai, God having given him the Law to give the people. Matthew shows that the people understood Moses as giver of the Law (Matt 19:7–9). After Moses succeeded in gaining Israel's freedom, he began to see the need for rules of government, and God fashioned these laws to guide Israel. No nation has existed without laws with which to govern; Israel was no different than other nations. Moses gave the Law to guide them as he received it from God. The nation of Israel needed pre-stated laws. The need for organized rules of government was realized (Exod 18:1–27).

Not only was Moses a good leader, intercessor, and lawgiver; he was a servant above servants. Moses is called "the servant of the Lord" in Deuteronomy 34:5. He is referred to as "the Lord, and his servant Moses."(Exod 14:31) God calls him "My servant Moses" in Numbers 12:7-8. Joshua calls him "the servant of the Lord" or variations of this expression 18 times. Throughout the rest of the Bible, this description is used 15 times. From these many references we understand that Moses was pleasing to the Lord. Moses truly possessed all the following characteristics of a servant of God: God upholds Moses before Aaron and Miriam (Num 12:1–8). Moses was chosen of God (Ps 106:23). God's spirit was upon him (Num 11:17; 25). God delighted in Moses (Num 11:10–15; 17–20). And the servant Moses would judge his people (Exod 18:13).

What was the role of the Servant of the Lord? Exodus 3:10 says that he was to be a leader. This is demonstrated throughout the Old Testament. Being a leader was the first task Moses was to accomplish. He was to teach about God and his will. This was demonstrated throughout the books of Exodus and Deuteronomy.

The servant was to be obedient. Moses demonstrated that through the Books of Moses (Exod. 25:1–40:38). In making the furnishings and the Tabernacle he did exactly as God told him—that is obedience. These characteristics are the reason God chose Moses to be His servant for the great task of making Israel into a great nation. He had the "right stuff."

Application

In a similar way the Hebrew writer demonstrates how a New Testament Christian should follow Moses' example, as portrayed in the book of Hebrews. By following Moses' examples, we can enjoy a relationship with Christ and God the Father. By doing this we set the strongest examples before the people we with whom come into contact. This is Christian living at its highest level. We know that God will count us faithful servants, same as he counted Moses, if we do our best and remain faithful. God will treat us the same because there is "no variableness, neither shadow of turning" (Jas 1:17).

Let us now look at the Apostle Paul and how he treats the subject of examples. Paul, speaking of Old Testament events, says, "Now all these things happened unto them for examples: and they are written for our admonition, upon whom the ends of the world are come" (1Cor 10:11). Some of these events related directly to Moses in the Exodus from Egypt. He also wrote in Romans 15:4, "For whatsoever things were written aforetime were written for our learning, that we through patience and comfort of the Scriptures might have hope." The word "example" means "a person or thing worthy of imitation. A model, a plan, etc. used in making things. A model or plan to be used in reproduction of the original." We, as Christians, are obligated to imitate or follow these examples in order to serve God as he desires us to do. Paul continued his instructions concerning following an example (2 Thess 3:9): "Not because we have not power, but to make ourselves an example unto you to follow us." Something or someone must be followed. Moses was an example in so many ways for us to follow.

When Moses was convinced, he obeyed God without question. He encouraged others to be the same. He is our example to imitate. This is proven by the many references throughout the Bible of his faith and obedience.

We, too, are to be examples to others in our service to Christ. That is what Christianity is all about. 1 Timothy 4:12 reads, "Let no man despise thy youth; but be thou an example of the believers, in word, in conversation, in charity, in spirit, in faith, in purity." Timothy was a minister; so are we. We must be examples to others in demonstrating just what following Christ really is.

Conclusion

Christians' faith should be strengthened by reading Hebrews 11 because of the repeated use of faith and God's positive response toward man's obedience. From this great chapter Moses gives us a strong example to strengthen our faith in God. Since God never changes, we trust he will respond accordingly toward us today. "For the promise is unto you, and to your children, and to all that are afar off, even as many as the Lord our God shall call" (Acts 2:39). Though this passage in Acts is referring to the gift of the Holy Spirit, the principle of God's rewarding us for our faithfulness is the same. Moses was called by God and we are called by the word of God, as recorded on the written pages which are given by inspiration of God. We will receive God's grace and favor if we keep a penitent heart and continue to grow in faith toward God and his holy word.

Discussion Questions
1. What aspects of Moses' life do you consider to be the greatest examples of faithfulness?
2. In what ways did Moses fail in his faithfulness, and how did he respond in those situations?
3. What aspects of Moses' life does the writer of Hebrews emphasize?

Rahab

Kirk Brothers

Focus Passages: Joshua 2:1–21; 6:15–25; Hebrews 11:31; James 2:24–25

One Main Thing: Rahab was not the only one in Jericho who believed in God, but she was the only one who would trust and obey.

Introduction

On March 11, 2011 a giant tsunami struck the eastern shore of Japan. Between the town of Rikuzen-Takata and the ocean once stood 70,000 red and black pines. After the massive wave struck land, the town was missing one third of its 23,300 residents, most of its buildings, and all but one of the pines that once stood as a protective barrier between the town and the ocean. A single 90-foot-tall, 200-year-old-tree remained. It lived for a year and a half after the salt inundated its root system and the earth it relied upon for nourishment. It was such a symbol of hope to the community and nation that a replica of the tree now stands where it once stood. This lesson focuses on another beacon of hope.

In Genesis 12, God made three promises to Abram (later Abraham) that serve as the outline of the Bible: (1) his descendants will be a great nation; (2) they will have a land of their own; and (3) through a seed of Abram all nations will be blessed. The New Testament highlights the fulfillment of the third promise (through Christ) and the Old Testament details the fulfillment of the first two promises (through Israel). The book of Joshua focuses on the second promise becoming a reality. It is in this book that we find the story of the rehab of Rahab and the wall that did not fall.

Going Deeper

Reality "survivor" shows were all the rage a few years ago. A person or a group of people would be dropped off in a remote and dangerous location and he/she/they would need to figure out how to survive and would often give instructions to viewers on how to do so as well. The story of Rahab is a story of survival.

Survivor Men

Our story begins with two survivor men, two spies sent out by Joshua. Israel crossed the Jordan River north of the Dead Sea. The first town they would encounter was Jericho. Archaeologists tell us that the town likely had two walls: an outer wall that was six-feet thick and an inner wall that was 12-feet thick. There was a fifteen-foot space between the two walls. Almost 40 years before Joshua sent out his spies, Moses sent twelve spies to infiltrate the land of Canaan. Ten spies gave a negative report but two gave a positive report which included trusting God to deliver the land into their hands. The people listened to the ten and spent the next 40 years wandering in the wilderness. Joshua was one of the two trusting spies. It is interesting, as the Israelites tried once again to invade the land, that Joshua only sent two spies. The sending of spies was strategic. Could it be that the sending of two spies was symbolic?

These two survivor men were smart. This is seen, for example, in the fact that they went to gather information in a place where people would likely ask few questions or want to identify who they saw there. **These men were strong.** They hid under flax. You may not think this is such a big deal but there is more to the story. Flax was largely imported from Egypt. The fibers of older plants were used for making rope and the fibers from younger plants were used for making linen. They would dry the plants and then take them through a "retting" process to separate out the fibers. The stalks were soaked in stagnant water and then laid out to dry. "The smell and sogginess would have made hiding here a distinctly unpleasant experience, perhaps equivalent to burying oneself in a pile of pig slops" (*IVP Old Testament Background Commentary*). The strength of the spies can also be seen in the fact they survived in hiding in the Judean desert for three days (cf. Josh 2:22). **The spies also saw success**. They trusted that God would give Israel the victory. When they returned to Joshua they said, "Surely the Lord has given all the land into our hands; moreover, all the inhabitants of the land have melted away before us" (Josh 2:24).

Survivor woman:

The heart of this story is not the survivor men but the survivor woman. The story of Rahab is shocking in many respects. **She was a woman with faults**. Rahab was a prostitute from a pagan, idol worshiping nation, yet, she was listed in the lineage of Jesus in Matthew 1:5–6 and was found in the faith hall of fame in Hebrews 11. Josephus and the Jewish Targums referred to her as an "innkeeper" but Scripture clearly refers to her as a prostitute (cf. Heb 11:31). She was a hero to the Jewish people so you can understand why Jewish writers might want to avoid mentioning her seedy side. It is likely that she was both an innkeeper and a prostitute.

We have already noted that her home would likely be a good place to gather information. Men who went there might not want others to know they were there and would be less likely to tell who they saw there. Having said that, there is something else we need to consider. It is interesting to me that when the king of the city sent his messengers, they did not break down Rahab's door and barge in. There is much we do not know about her culture, but it is puzzling that the king thinks spies are in her house, yet he only asks her to send them out. There might be several reasons for this, but one is particularly intriguing. At least one scholar has proposed the idea that maybe she was a temple prostitute. We do know that these existed in some ancient cultures. If so, she would have been viewed as a holy person in some sense (a priestess) and thus the king may have been reluctant to barge in. At the end of the day, we do not know with certainty why the king proceeded the way he did.

Many people note that Rahab lied in response to the king's request (cf. 2:4–6). She lied about knowing where they were, and she hid them from the king and his agents. Some are bothered by this because she is listed as a hero of faith and yet lying is inappropriate for God's people. There are a couple of thoughts that are worth highlighting here. First of all, Rahab had come to believe that the God of Israel was a true and powerful God, but her faith was a new and immature faith. She did not have a full understanding of the morality of those who follow God. Having said this, we also need to recognize that the spies, who did understand the morality God expects of his people, encouraged her to continue the lie and even made it a requirement for her survival. It is important to realize that this takes place in a time of war. The Israelites were about to attack. Deception is at the heart of warfare. You do not want the enemy to know what you are doing. The whole concept of a spy implies deception. Spies hid and deceived in order to gather information. To conclude from this that it is ok for us to lie to our spouse, our boss, or our neighbor or to cheat on our taxes is completely inappropriate.

Rahab was also a woman with faith. She told the spies that the hearts of the people of Jericho had melted because of the great things they heard that God had (parting of Red Sea, defeat of two Amorite kings). Rahab declared that "the Lord your God, He is God in heaven above and on earth beneath" (Josh 2:11). This was a simple declaration of faith. She had much to learn about the nature of God and what it means to follow him. Yet, this was also real faith. She had heard enough about the God of Israel to risk everything based on trust in Hm. It is worth noting that Rahab was not the only one in Jericho who believed that the God of Israel was real. The hearts of all the people melted because of their belief. Yet, she was the only one willing to trust and obey. She trusted God over her king, her city walls, her army, and her gods. Rahab also obeyed. She did exactly what the spies requested. She not only hid them, helped them escape, and told them what to do when they left the city, she kept their secret. Believing that God was real and powerful was not enough. She had to act on that faith, and she did.

Finally, Rahab was a woman who cared about her family. She made sure that her family was included in the cloak of protection. There would have been risk involved in this. Would the spies think this was too much? Saving one woman was one thing. Saving an entire family was another. Her faith in God and her love for her family paid off. They agreed to her request. Two things were required. First of all, safety was extended to her home alone and all family members must be in that house. Secondly, she must mark her home with a single scarlet thread hanging from the window. We again see that her faith was an active faith. This is why James declared, "And in the same way was not Rahab the harlot also justified by works, when she received the messengers and sent them out by another way?" (2:25)

Application

Rahab and her family survived because she trusted God, obeyed God, shared salvation with her family, and made sure her family was in the one house to which God's grace was extended. Are we willing to put our trust in God, and will we put that faith into action through obedience? (Jas 2:18-26) God's grace extends to those who are in Christ Jesus (Rom 3:24; 5:1-2). Are we in Him? (cf. Gal 3:26-27) Are we part of His people? (Col 1:21-23) Have we shared the good news of salvation in Christ with our families? (Eph 6:1-4; Acts 10:23-24) Have we brought them into the place of safety?

Conclusion

Hurricane Ike ravaged the town of Gilchrist, Texas, in September of 2008. One section of 200 homes was completely wiped out, except for a single yellow house belonging to Warren and Pam Adams. Cut to Joshua 6. On the seventh day of their marching around the walls of Jericho, the Israelites circled the city seven times. This would likely have lulled the inhabitants of Jericho into apathy. Suddenly, the trumpets blasted, the people shouted, and the great walls came crashing down. The blood curdling cries of the invading army mixed with the trumpets' echoes, the cries of terror, and the explosive crash of the walls which shook the ground; the commotion would have overwhelmed the last defenses of the people of Jericho whose hearts had already melted long before the Israelites came rushing into their city.

As the dust began to clear, a single remaining chunk of wall begins to take shape against the backdrop of the ruble. One lone house is still standing... a house with a simple scarlet thread hanging from the window. Though it has no voice with which to speak, this house speaks nonetheless. It speaks of the impact of a woman who trusted the God of Israel and loved her family enough to risk everything. She trusted and obeyed, and her house stood as a beacon of faith and hope. It was the wall that did not fall. When the final trumpet call sounds and the Son of God sweeps down from the sky with His mighty angels, may our faith and the faith of our families be standing as well!

Discussion:
1. How might the culture of Jericho have been different from the culture of Israel?
2. What are some of the challenges that Rahab would have faced as she made decisions in response to the invasion of the Israelites?
3. What challenges would she have faced as she lived among the Israelites after the battle?
4. How might the events of Acts 10:23–38 compare to Rahab bringing her family into her home?
5. What is the most valuable thing you have learned from this lesson?

Barak

Arvy Dupuy

Focus Passage: Hebrews 11:32
One Main Thing: Barak followed God's unusual plans rather than his own.

Introduction

Who was Barak and what did he do that led to his inclusion in a list of biblical heroes like Samson, David and Samuel? What lesson from his life do we need to learn?

Barak's story is full of unexpected twists and turns. There are violations of cultural norms and traditional roles, unlikely heroes—or heroines!—and a stereotypical protagonist assigned a minor role. That is the story of Barak in Judges 4. The cycle of deliverance, regression, pain and a cry for deliverance by judges again repeats itself as the chapter begins. The general picture of that period of Israelite history is one of continued tension with biblical faith, as the new Israelite settlers in Canaan found them-selves alternately repelled by certain aspects of the indigenous culture and enticed by others. Israel cannot make up their mind. They cannot settle into a consistent and theologically acceptable pattern of living.

Three times prior, the same series of events had occurred. Then, as now, time and the lack of generational education led Israel to return to old habits and previous outcomes. In Judges 4 God takes another path, possibly to try and gain the attention of Israel, probably to remind them He is still in control and operates as He wills, how He wills, and uses who we might see as the least likely people to accomplish His purposes.

Going Deeper

Our primary text in Hebrews 11 where Barak's name is dropped drives us back to the Old Testament, where we find out who he was and why he merited such high recognition. The first three verses of Judges 4 set the scene. In v. 4 we are introduced to Deborah, a prophetess and judge. She summons Barak to deal with the Canaanite oppressor, and here is where Barak's character begins to show up. Inside the families of that time, women were the primary cogs in the production of goods necessary for everyday life, but that status did not translate to leadership roles outside the household. That is why Deborah's position and her request was so unusual. However, Barak's response tells us of his respect for her and probably his regard for women in general. This commander of men goes to the wise woman under the tree. Absent from beginning to end in this narrative is any tension regarding society's view of the role of men and women. Nevertheless, the tension was present, as we will see. The people desperately needed deliverance. Economics and survival were at the heart of the conflict. It is in the context of these elements that Barak and Deborah came together to free their people in a war of liberation that carried historical significance for generations to come.

In vv. 6-7 Deborah lays out the overall plan: attack and eliminate the threat. Barak's response to this demonstrates his understanding of what the problem is and is not. Too often our human nature moves us to see barriers to dealing with the real problem. Think about all the objections Barak could have brought up at this point. A woman in charge? Attacking a seasoned army with nine hundred chariots and no doubt more of the latest technology in warfare? An Israelite army with limited weaponry? None of this made sense. But so often faith, real faith, does not make sense. That is what the writer of Hebrews lays out as the great faith chapter begins. Barak does not become distracted by any of these or other qualifiers. His faith in Deborah, and God, move him to respond in the affirmative (v. 8).

Up to this point his reactions have been remarkable, but then in what might be seen as one last test, Deborah tells him he will not receive any glory for his actions. He can go and risk his life; he can risk the lives of his men but someone else will get the glory. We hold our breath to see what his response will be, but the text shows no hint of hesitation—off they go to battle, these two unlikely allies.

The engagement point is at the Kishon River, a perfect place for Barak's faith to pay off in the form of a rainstorm that caused it to flood. This bogged down and neutralized those nine hundred Canaanite chariots and, for that matter, their infantry, in a sea of mud. The result was a bloody rout for the Canaanites, climaxing when Sisera abandoned his chariot and fled on foot to take shelter in Jael's tent.

Here we see a stark contrast to Barak. Sisera mirrors the men of that time and their attitudes, and treatment, toward women. When he receives refuge and refreshment from Jael, he still barks instructions to her. He tells her where to stand and what to say (v. 20). She showed kindness and he gave orders. No doubt Jael had to wonder what would happen to her when he awoke from his nap. Sisera saw Jael for who he wanted her to be, someone who did what he wanted. Barak saw Deborah for who she was, a messenger of God. The contrast is startling, and the end is what we want it to be. The man who disrespected the woman got a tent peg in the head, courtesy of the woman. And the man who respected the woman got his name included in a long list of Biblical heroes.

Application

Seldom does real life have such a happy ending. This narrative that began so out of the ordinary ends so perfectly, but we have to wait to the true end. By the end of the battle there is little doubt that Barak was a national hero. However, Deborah took center stage. In Judges 5 we come to the victory song. These were common in the day and served the dual purpose of a record of the events and a celebration of the achievement. For Israel they typically honored God but also extolled the central operative. The song includes Barak, but he shares secondary billing with two other women, one of whom is the mother of the defeated Canaanite general. Five hundred years later he is included in a list of Israelite deliverers (1 Sam 12:11). Later, Hebrews has him in pretty elite company.

This text is such a reflection of life and faith and how the story ends, in the true end.

Life is seldom as it should be or as we think it should be. There are always so many curves and variables. Life has a way of calling an audible when we least expect and when times are at their worst.

Israel was in desperate need of a hero, a rescuer, and it came in a way that no one expected. Barak's attitude throughout this saga demonstrates his faith. There is no way it worked out the way he thought it would. When he and his men were sitting around the campfire talking about what "someone needs to do" about the Canaanite problem, there is little doubt that anyone said, "A woman should take care of it." But nowhere in the text is there even a suggestion that Barak was mad, angry, hurt, or felt slighted by what did occur.

Far too often at the beginning of our faith we walk so strong—our vision is clear, our focus is set on God, and our hearts are all in. Then without warning, things begin to go in a different direction than we had planned. Events play out in a version not consistent with our vision, people do not cooperate with our objectives, and, if we are not careful, pride will begin to rise up. What happens, even before we realize it, is that everything shifts, and it becomes all about us. When it takes hold of our lives, we are prevented from being all God wants us to be by blinding us to His ways. It tempts us to believe that we know better than He does, that our plans, ways, path are best. I am sure Barak had plans. It would seem logical that this leader had been having discussions with his lieutenants about how to deal with the Canaanite issue. However, God was way ahead of him, preparing a most unlikely solution, and he trusted God and followed His lead.

Anne Graham Lotz, in her book, *Heaven: My Father's House*, tells the story of an old missionary named Samuel Morrison and his wife, who had spent twenty-five years doing ministry in Africa. They returned to America on the same ocean liner that brought

President Teddy Roosevelt back from a hunting expedition in Africa. When the ship docked, President Roosevelt was bombarded with masses of people welcoming him home from his hunting expedition. Police were needed to keep the throng from rushing the President. The Morrisons disembarked, also. Walking off the ship alone, no one greeted them; they couldn't even hail a cab for a ride. Later, a in small rented room Morrison complained to God out loud. "The president was in Africa hunting for three weeks, killing animals for sport and the whole world turns out to welcome him home. We have given twenty-five years of our lives in Africa, serving You, and, finally, worn out and sick, we come home, and no one has greeted us or even knows we are here." On hearing this, his wife replied to him, "Samuel, we are not home yet!"[1]

Conclusion

Be faithful to the end, all the way to the end. God will make it right. He will honor you and your trust in Him. And you will make the list, the only list that matters.

Discussion Questions

1. What problem are you facing in your life right now? What is the last place or person you would think could help you solve that problem? Write that person's name down and pray for them.
2. Can you think of a time in your life where God surprised you with an unlikely outcome? Discuss that with the group.

---

[1] Lotz, Anne Graham, *Heaven: My Father's House* (Nashville, Nelson, 2001).

3. Has there been a time in your life when you have seen someone, other than yourself, do all the work and someone else take the credit? Based on your observations, how did the person slighted handle it?

Gideon
Philip Goad

Focus passage: Hebrews 11:32–34
One Main Thing: When Gideon first appears in Scripture, he possesses a powerful name but not a powerful faith. Yet a patient and merciful God helps him grow past his fears to become a mighty warrior, a person of faith later described by the Hebrew as one of those who "from weakness were made strong" (Heb. 11:34). The same unchanging God can help us grow past our fears too!

Introduction

What would you attempt to do if you were not afraid of failure? Most of us can think of something we haven't attempted because of not wanting to fail. NBA legend Michael Jordan stated, "I've missed more than 9000 shots in my career. I've lost almost 300 games. 26 times, I've been trusted to take the last shot...and missed. I've failed over and over and over again in my life. And that is why I succeed." Great athletes always want the ball in their hands. Yes, an opportunity to fail, but they have a confidence born out of knowing that they must risk failure to win.

Consider another version of the question: What would you be willing to do for God if you were not afraid of failure—especially if God personally asked you to serve? The story of Gideon helps us understand that our fears shouldn't prevent us from stepping forward in faith to serve. It also helps us understand that with God's help, we can grow past our fears.

Going Deeper

Israel is in the promised land, but it isn't all good. In fact, it's bad. In taking the land, Israel hadn't completely driven out the inhabitants of the land (Judg 1:28). Just as God had warned them, the influence of those not in a covenant relationship with God have caused Israel's attention to be diverted from the one true God to false gods (Judg 2:11-12). Compounding the problem, the Israelites have neglected to teach God's covenant to their children. As a result, God has allowed some nations to remain for the testing of Israel (Judg 3:4). And so, as Scripture introduces the judges, it also introduces us to an ongoing cycle of sin followed by repentance during those times when a judge is leading the people.

Judges 6 introduces us to Gideon during the sin cycle. For seven years the Midianites have been oppressing Israel; severe to the point that Israel has cried out to the Lord for help (Judg 6:6). God's first response is to send a prophet who reminds Israel that the reason for their current situation is that they have not obeyed God (Judg 6:6-10).

However, God's grace and mercy are on display as he sends an angel to recruit Gideon. We find Gideon beating out wheat in a wine press to hide the food from the Midianites (Judg 6:11-13). The greeting from this angel of the Lord should have inspired confidence. Instead, Gideon's response is a question: "If the Lord is with us, why has all of this (oppression) happened to us?" In other words, "If God is with us, why I am I beating out wheat in a wine press?" Gideon is blaming God and in doing so, reveals that he is ignorant of God's covenant. He's heard some of the great God-stories of the past but doesn't seem to understand that Israel's negative circumstances are their own fault. It is easy to sense both his fear and his frustration.

The Lord again encourages Gideon to step up and lead, but Gideon needs to be convinced (Judg 6:14-16). He makes it about himself by making excuses. "Are you sure you have the right guy here? My family is the least in Manasseh, and I'm the youngest in my father's house." It's interesting that Gideon has a powerful name but not a powerful faith. His name means "feller" or "warrior," but he is dominated by fear.

Although flawed and fearful, Gideon isn't shy when it comes to asking. He asks the angel of the Lord for a sign to prove this message is really from God. Thankfully, a patient God is ready to help Gideon grow. Gideon hurriedly makes a meal and sets it before the angel of the Lord (Judg 6:20-21). Instead of eating the meal, the angel touches the food with his staff and fire springs from the rock and consumes it. Then the angel of the Lord vanishes. God is helping Gideon grow. Gideon responds by worshiping God (Judg 6:22-24).

On the same night, God challenges Gideon by asking him to pull down "the altar of Baal that belongs to your father" (Judg 6:25-27). Gideon obeys but does so under the cover of darkness. His fear at this point isn't about failure as much as it is about his own safety. God's challenge: Loyal to me or loyal to family? Will you stand for me by standing up to your family? Will you trust me enough to obey me when doing so is scaring you to death? Gideon still has fears. No way we would regard his faith as confident so far, but he's growing—and God is with him.

Gideon survives the Baal incident, and Judges 6 concludes with Gideon asking God for two more signs. It's as if Gideon is asking, "God, is this really going to be me plus you?" Gideon first requests that God allow there to be dew on a fleece that he will leave out overnight but not on the threshing floor. On the next night Gideon asks God to reverse the sign; a dry fleece but dew on the threshing floor. God's patience and grace is again on display as he provides Gideon with the requested signs (Judg 6:36–40).

Before Gideon takes on Midian, God whittles down the Israelite army to ensure that everyone understands that this victory is about him and not about the strength of Gideon and the army (Judg 7:2). It's interesting because the numbers are already daunting: 32,000 Israelites to take on some 135,000 Midianites. To decrease the size of the army, God's instructs Gideon to tell the scared soldiers to go home. As a result, 22,000 leave, but the army of 10,000 is still too large. Next God instructs Gideon to administer a water-drinking test and cuts the number to just 300! The numbers are now 135,000 versus 300—seemingly absurd! Imagine filling up your favorite major college football stadium including seating on the playing field and then having an army about the size of the university marching band fight them!

After drastically reducing the size of the army, our amazing and merciful God provides one more sign for his chosen leader. God sends Gideon down to the Midianite camp, and Gideon overhears the enemy talking about a dream. The interpretation of the dream is that God is giving Midian into the hand of Gideon! (Judg 7:9–14) Gideon offers worship to God and returns to the Israelite camp as the confident leader God wants him to be (Judg 7:15).

With confidence and faith, Gideon then leads his small army against Midian.

Application

How can we grow in faith by becoming less fearful and more confident?

1. Allow the Gideon story to motivate us and assure us! Gideon possessed a powerful name (Feller) but life had left him fearful and hiding in a wine press. God's patience is on display as he offers sign after sign to Gideon, and Gideon grows up spiritually.

The name "Christian" suggests to the world that we are following Christ. It is inappropriate to follow in a covert way or to operate from a position of fear. Thankfully in the United States, it is unusual to face the kinds of fears that challenged both Gideon and first-century Christians. Our goal should be to possess the boldness and confidence possessed by disciples when the church was brand new. Confidence like that of Peter and John should motivate us (Acts 4:13, and we should be pleading for the same kind of confidence our brethren did (Acts 4:29).

2. When tempted to ask, "Will God plus me work?" try to remember that even though Gideon is asking that question, it isn't a great question. Why? The Gideon story and many others remind us that it is always about God and never about the person through whom God chooses to accomplish his purpose. God drives this idea home with Gideon and all the people by whittling down Gideon's army to a group that could never win without divine intervention.

3. When tempted to ask God, "Why me?" regarding a particular area of service, develop the courage to ask a better question.

Choose instead to ask, "Why not me?" Imagine the amount of good God could accomplish through us once we embrace this mindset! Imagine developing the "God plus me" confidence to dive into a new area of ministry, to teach that first Bible class, to share the life-changing good news about Jesus with your friends. Imagine God accomplishing something through you that your own vision never would have been broad enough to see!

When we resist offering ourselves for service, is it possible that it's a trust issue for us? If so, we have another powerful reminder of why the Gideon lesson is so valuable. In the beginning he isn't confident and has his fears, but he is mentioned in Hebrews 11 when we are reminded of all those people of faith. What an encouragement this should be for all of us! Sometimes we need more strength than we could ever find on our own. Gideon helps us understand why God wants and can always use a confident faith from us.

Conclusion:

Obviously, there will still be some days when we are weak and fearful. In those moments, it would be amazing to be able to ask God for a sign like Gideon did. In those moments, I would challenge us remember, arguably, our most important blessing. We are blessed in that God has given us a sign—his most powerful sign ever and one that stands the test of time. And, guys like Gideon didn't have it. God's most powerful sign is the empty tomb! And it's so much more than a sign; it makes heaven possible for us!

I asked at the beginning: What would you be willing to do for God if you were not afraid of failure—especially if God personally asked you to serve? Always remember, God has personally invited us to serve. Service is the purpose for which he saved us! Thanks be to God for sharing Gideon's story of transformation with us!

Discussion Questions

1. Does Gideon seem to you like a good example of faithfulness? In what ways?

2. What are some ways in which Gideon falls short as an example of faithfulness?

Sawn in Two
Jeremy W. Barrier

Focus passage: Hebrews 11:36–40

One Main Thing: Learning to trust God is a life-long pursuit for some of us. However, for some it is not. There are people in the world who not only spend their lives developing their faith in God, but in some cases, they have given up their lives in faith to God. We call these disciples of God "martyrs," a special group of people who have lived *and* died for the Lord Jesus Christ.

The Youth Rally is Over! (the following is based on true events)

Ho Van Nguyen[1] sat down at the booth, picked up his small espresso-sized coffee cup and proceeded to down the mixture of finely ground coffee grains, water, sugar cane granules, and hot, steamed milk, boiled into a froth. His eyes stared at me intently as he finished his morning cup. While being 54 years old, he looked at least a decade older, as he peered into my eyes through the caverns of carefully crafted and squinted brows that reminded me of smooth parallel shaped rock formations somewhere in Utah. Nguyen's eyes and face told me that his life had been hard. As I sat, I anticipated the story that he was about to unfold within my mind's eye. Nguyen was a Christian who had lived through the overthrow of South Vietnam in 1975, when the North Vietnamese established their socialist, anti-Christian government throughout the entire nation. His story went something like this.

---

[1] Names of individuals have been changed for their protection.

"I was 23 years old. A minister for a church in Vinh Long and I loved my family, my Jesus, and my church. It had been 3 years since the change of governments had taken place. I had already been interviewed, interrogated, 're-educated', and I was trying to move forward. The greatest blow for me was the state of the church. Since the government had cracked down on 'illegal' Christian groups, we had largely been dispersed and scattered, and meetings became fewer and farther between. I, with a few of my youth minister friends, had decided that we were going to try to have a youth rally. A youth rally that would be city-wide! We made meticulously detailed plans on how we would disseminate the news of the meeting. Then, we did it. We spread the word from house to house and church to church, quietly, carefully, and deliberately. Finally, after a period of approximately a month's time, the event was upon us! Slowly, but surely, people began to come. There were 10, then 20, then 50, even up to 100 were present! We were so excited as everyone filed in, one by one, to begin the first youth rally that we had been a part of in over 5 years! Finally, it was decided that everyone who would come had arrived, and we were just on the verge of leading our opening prayer, when suddenly the power to the entire building was turned off. Within seconds, there was shouting from outside, people began to rise, scatter, tossing chairs, screaming, and from every perceivable entrance to the building, I could see the police. Knowing that I had been the one to organize the event, I knew there would be no sense in running. I sat down. I waited and remained calm, as I was completely aware that not only the meeting would not be taking place, but we had been betrayed. Betrayed by an infiltrator, for the sum of money that would probably buy an individual one meal or maybe two. So much hope. So much trust in God. The result? Failure."

Going Deeper

In the book of Hebrews, God has transmitted his Divine Word to us through the voice and words of a preacher. The text of Hebrews represents a fantastic sermon, probably delivered within an assembly of faith located in or around Alexandria, Egypt, sometime between the years 60 and 90 AD representing a persuasive defense of how and why one should remain loyal to Jesus Christ our Lord and to His Church. As the sermon reaches a fever pitch of excitement and *crescendo* toward the end of the writing, his homily escalates into a passage of thought that details the "who's who" of faith; often times called a "hall of fame" of faith! After detailing so many of the heroes from the Scriptures, the preacher finally comes to the end, where a word is left for those who are not only named in Scripture, but even those who are not. In a similar way to the "tomb of the unknown soldier", the Hebrew writer highlights those who not only lived their lives trusting the promises of God, but even highlights those who lived *and died*—cruel deaths in some cases—yet persevered in their trust of God to *deliver them!*

One such example is one who is mentioned in Hebrews 11:37 who was "sawn assunder". Scholars have attempted to identify who is being referred to within this passage. There is one story of a Jew who was resisting the Romans as they were laying siege to

Jerusalem in the late 60s AD. The Romans grabbed him, clamped him to a sawhorse and sawed in two. Another story relates how some Jews from Cyrene in the early second century were taken and sawn in two from the head downwards. However, while such stories are obviously difficult, and would have called to mind the faithfulness of Israel to God, as all of the named heroes of faith in chapter eleven, most scholars have come to the conclusion that the hero who was sawn in two was most likely Isaiah, the prophet of Jerusalem. While the death of the famous prophet is not related within the text of Isaiah itself, later traditions do record the supposed death of the prophet. After Isaiah had denounced the wicked King Manasseh, he was ordered to be cut in two. One tradition even tells of how Isaiah, in an attempt to flee and escape the wrath of Manasseh, hid within a hollowed-out Cedar tree, only to be taken in the tree, when his pursuers cut the tree in half, thus killing Isaiah in the process.

Of course, the emphasis of the Hebrews passage points to a reality that plagued the early church. Some of the earliest disciples, as they were "witnesses" to the life and events of Jesus, even remained faithful to their testimony to the point of persecution, trials, and eventual death. These faithful believers are those we call the "martyrs"—those who lived their lives faithful to God even to the point of death! An early church leader of North Africa by the name of Tertullian is famous for having made the claim "The blood of the martyrs is the seed of the church."

Jesus is found in such passages as Mark 13, giving instructions to His disciples on how to face trials and persecutions, and how they should handle themselves and respond! What is Jesus' basic answer paraphrased? Trust God! First Peter devotes a large portion of the text encouraging those who face trials for the faith (1 Pet 1:1–7). A major emphasis of the book of Revelation entertains the idea of how God will bring justice for the faithful martyrs who were faithful, even to the point of dying for the faith (Rev 2:10–13; 6:9–11; 20:4). In a similar fashion, the Hebrew preacher notes in Hebrews 12:4, "Ye have not resisted unto blood, striving against sin." The thought itself in this passage is both reassuring and foreboding! While they have seen periods of trial, is it possible that they might have to hold to their trust in God to the point of shedding blood? In the same context, the looming reality is always present, knowing that Jesus ultimately did shed his blood and died in his faithfulness and trust in the Almighty. Wow! What a compelling and awe-inspiring sermon!

Application

The way of faith is sometimes a lifelong journey. Sometimes it is not. Sometimes our lives are cut short. Sometimes the lives of those we love around us are cut short. How is your faith even in those circumstances? Do you look with eyes of trust to your heavenly Father to abide with you, be with you, comfort you, and strengthen you, even when the trials become immense? This is the theme, the challenge, and the exhortation of the Hebrew preacher who so powerfully encourages us to "Have Faith" and "Trust God!"

Conclusion

Nguyen was arrested that day. After his arrest, he along with several others were interrogated, tested, re-educated, and ultimately carried out a 6-month prison sentence for their crime. The prison cell held approximately 100 inmates in an area of about 25 ft. x 25 ft. There was no climate control and temperatures were consistently above 90 degrees Fahrenheit. However, he persisted. He endured. He trusted God. To this day, Nguyen is my friend, fellow brother in Christ, and lives a life trusting in his Lord as he is faithful…faithful even unto death, if he is called to such an end.

Discussion

1. Which hero of Israel was "sawn in two" for his trust in God?
2. Who is a martyr?
3. Are we called to live our lives to God in trust of Him and His Word? Are we called to give even our lives for the faith?
4. Several passages of the New Testament deal with those who have suffered for the faith (e.g., Rev 6:9–11; 20:4). How will God deal with these people in the end?

Samson

Travis Harmon

Focus Passage: Hebrews 11:32

One Main Thing: The heroes of faith listed in Hebrews 11 are commended for having confidence in something they could not see to the point that they acted on that belief. We need to have a faith that causes us to act.

Introduction

It's the hall of fame of faith! This is one of the most well-known chapters in all of the Bible. People know that Hebrews 11 is the hall of fame of faith like they know that 1 Corinthians 13 is the great chapter on love, that Genesis 1 is the creation, that Acts 2 is the establishment of the church, and that Proverbs 31 is the chapter about the virtuous woman.

Just look at those names! It is truly a who's who of the heroes of the Old Testament! Abel, Enoch, Noah, Abraham, Sarah, Isaac, Jacob, Joseph, Moses, Rahab, Gideon, Barak, and Samson … hold on there. What are these two doing there in the list of the heroes of faith? Samson? Rahab? Rahab was a prostitute that lied and Samson? Do you remember his story?

What is he doing there? Have you read of him? What is this clown doing here with the likes of Abraham and Joseph?

Going Deeper

Samson's story is NOT a kid's story. I think most of us only ever hear the sanitized kid's version of Samson from VBS; most of those VBS stories celebrate Samson as the "Strong Man." If you want to know the real story, you need to go back to Judges 13-16.

Chapter 13 is the story of Samson's birth. Manoah and his wife are told they will have a son, and they wisely ask how they should raise the child. Hebrews 11 should have them listed because of their faith and actions. Samson was to be raised a Nazarite, a term that indicates "consecrated or separated" and required abstinence from grapes, from having his hair cut, and from becoming ritually impure through contact with something dead (see Num 6). If you know the story at all, you see all of this is going to be a problem.

Read chapters 14-16 and see if Samson is not a clown. The first time we meet Samson (14:2-3), he is asking his parents to get him a Philistine woman as a wife because he says, "She pleases me well!" If you need a reminder, there is no greater enemy to God's people at this time than the Philistines.

Then we have this odd story about how he comes across a lion and kills it with his hands (14:5-9) because the "Spirit of the Lord came on him mightily" (that is a key phrase as noted in 14:6, 19; 15:14; 16:20). This leads to his ridiculous riddle (14:14) his first betrayal by a woman (14:15-17), his outlandish revenge using 300 foxes (15:4-5), and ultimately to his silly lyrics about killing 1000 people with the jawbone of a donkey (15:15-16).

Samson spends the night with a prostitute at the start of chapter 16, and the Philistines plan to attack in the morning. He gets up before them and carries off the gates of the city almost 40 miles back to Judah.

Then we get to Samson and Delilah (16:4). Three times they play out the same well-known scene (16:5–14). She begs for the answer to his strength, and when he tells her, she attempts to turn him over to the Philistines. She puts him to sleep and ties him with fresh bowstrings and new ropes, and then weaves his hair in a loom. Finally, he tells her, "I have been a Nazarite from birth" (16:17). Oh really? He says that a razor has never cut his hair, and that is the key to his strength. Again, Delilah lulls him to sleep and has his hair shorn and calls for the Philistines. He expected to get up like always; however, the Lord had left him. It had to be a shock to him. He broke all the vows, yet nothing had ever hurt him. They put his eyes out and made him grind grain (16:21). *Out of the eater something to eat. Out of the strong something sweet.*

They praise their God (16:23–25), and they bring Samson out as a spectacle. He prays for strength to take revenge for… his eyes! Then he pushes with all his might and collapses the building, killing more Philistines at one time then he had in his entire life. That is the story of Samson. A hero of faith?

Interpretation

After looking at the stories it is hard to understand why he is listed in Hebrews 11. In VBS, he is the "strong man," but it really appears more like he is a circus clown. God is certainly the hero; He is the strength. It was His spirit that helped Samson. In a lot of ways, a reading of Samson's story as a comedy seems appropriate. A read-through considering Jewish comedy makes Samson's story easier to interpret. Samson was a clown, **but he was a clown that trusted in God.**

Application

Samson and Rahab feel out of place. We focus on Rahab the *harlot* who *lied*, but she believed God would help his people defeat Jericho. "Before the spies lay down for the night, she went up on the roof and said to them, 'I know that the Lord has given you this land ... for the Lord your God is God in heaven above and on the earth below'" (Josh 2:8–9).

She had faith. That's why she's commended, not for her previous mistakes. "Now faith is being sure of what we hope for. And certain of what we do not see. This is what the ancients were commended for" (Heb 11:1–2). Her commendation arose from the fact that she had faith in something she could not see, and she acted on it. Her commendation is not a wholesale endorsement of her past actions or even how she went about her plan. We sometimes get bogged down thinking about what was wrong with her life and forget what was right.

Samson is the same way. The reader often considers his stories, seeing the bad choices and his ridiculous actions. However, he made a request and knew God would help. He "pushed with all his might" and trusted God to do the rest.

Conclusion

Out of place. Do you ever feel that way? Have you ever felt that way in church? Do you ever wonder, "What am I, a sinner and a clown, doing here with all of these good people of faith?" Do you ever feel like people just focus on your bad choices and ridiculous actions, and you just want to quit? You are not out of place in church! The word church really means "group or assembly." You are not out of place in Jesus's group! That is what the book of Hebrews is all about. In Hebrews 10, the writer tells us that Jesus died to take away our sins (10:5–10), and that we should not give up because we belong with Him (10:19–23). We will be rewarded if we have faith and confidence to keep that faith (10:35–39)! We just have to have faith in Him. Not that we are good enough, but that HE is good enough.

Without faith it is impossible to please him (Heb 11:6). Me please God? How is that possible? That's what I want to do—please Him. We just have to know He is and diligently seek Him.

I am not the strong man, and I am not the hero. Jesus is. I am just a clown ... I think people who know my backstory would say, "What is this clown doing here teaching others about the Bible?"

When I was in high school, I was on the cross-country team. I was the absolute worst runner on the team and one of the worst runners in the state. I was constantly racing to "just not be dead last." However, we went to the state sectional cross-country meet, and my team won. I got a trophy even though I personally finished almost dead last.

I know people were looking at me and saying, "What is that clown doing there?" What was I doing there? I was getting my trophy for winning a sectional cross country meet because I was on the right team, and I never quit the team. That is Hebrews 12:1—He is the finisher. We just need to be on the same team and never quit.

Discussion Questions:

1. How have people made you feel out of place before at any time in your life? At church?
2. What can we do to make sure people who come to meet with the church do not feel like outsiders or visitors, but rather that they know they are wanted in the group that we call church?
3. Is just having faith enough or do we need to DO something to be saved? How do you know action is required from Hebrews chapter 12? How does the Hebrew writer show he had faith?

Samuel
Nathan Guy

Focus Passage: Hebrews 11:32

Introduction

"And Jesus grew in wisdom, and stature, and in favor with God and man."

C. S. Lewis once was asked what he thought about gambling. He said he didn't think much of it because he knew nothing about it and was hopelessly bad at it. Said Lewis, "If anyone comes to me asking to play bridge for money, I just say 'how much do you hope to win? Take it, and go away.'"[1]

I can't help but feel the same way when, in the light of this text, I'm asked "how God grew in favor with God?" I'm tempted to reply 'what do want me to say? Pretend that I've said it and leave me alone!"

I suppose a careful study of the context would reveal that Luke has in mind the fulfillment of prophecy, and the uniqueness of Christ. I suppose there is much here that draws our vision to the One like no other, the perfect man who grows from grace to grace, on a road to which he was destined. God growing in favor with God is a powerful and awesome thought.

---

[1] C. S. Lewis, "Answers to Questions on Christianity [1944]" in *God in the Dock: Essays on Theology and Ethics* (Grand Rapids: Eerdmans, 1996), 60.

I hope you'll forgive me if I skip that hard question. But can we look into the eyes of my Lord, follow his steps, and answer his call? Can we be like him in any way, in any way remotely possible so that we, too, may grow in favor with God? Can I learn something about my own feeble walk with God by turning all attention to the boy who's come to the Temple? I believe the answer is yes. Yes, a thousand times yes. He is so infinitely more than my example…but he is my example no less. In this moment of worship, in the presence of the Holy One, we ask, O God, can we be like Christ and grow in favor with you? If so, speak Lord, your servants are listening.

Going Deeper

Right there on the pages of my Bible rest these words: "he grew in favor with God." Just one chapter earlier, we hear the beautiful prayer of his mother, as she cries out "My soul magnifies the Lord" and dedicates her son to God. The reader knows that the man of the house is not really his father, but he plays a father-figure role. The boy is a man of God, and shows himself to be so, even at a young age. There he is—pictured in the house of the Lord, training himself in the law. We hear in a story from his youth that he learns to bypass all other voices—even the voice of his father-figure, to recognize the one who called him to this task. And how does the Bible describe our young hero? Surrounded by priests given the official role of teaching the law, our hero stands heads and shoulders above those men, recognizing whose house this is, and just what calling he possesses. "He grew in stature, and in favor with God and man."

Stories about Jesus are riveting and exciting. They remind us of His uniqueness, but—you say—I find it so hard to apply them to me.

Good thing this isn't a story about Jesus.

The story I just told you concerns Samuel, the boy priest, in the first book that bears his name. And yet, it's not a coincidence that when Luke opens his magnificent gospel, he tells a story that sounds so familiar. The last man to serve as both prophet and priest over God's people is long gone and sorely missed. And yet…in this boy Jesus, prophet, priest, and king all meet.

How did Samuel grow in favor with God? If you read 1 Samuel 2 very carefully, you'll find two verses that serve as bookends: verse 21 states "the boy Samuel grew up in the presence of the Lord" and verse 26 is the memorable one: "he grew in stature and in favor with God and man." It just so happens, Luke 2 also gives us bookends: Before the Temple scene, verse 40 tells us "the child grew and became strong, filled with wisdom; and the favor of God was upon him," while verse 52 is the verse we all know.

So, if those are the bookends, what's in-between? We all know the Luke story—in-between is the boy Jesus in the Temple. But the Samuel story is very telling. Between the bookends that parallel Luke's narrative is a report. It seems that Eli's real sons are not acting like their father. They don't respect their father; and the text sadly reports "they would not listen to the voice of their father." But Samuel did. He acted more like a son to Eli (God's representative on earth) than Eli's own children. And thus, Samuel grew in favor with God. You must remember that this all takes place at the tabernacle in Shiloh; the tent of meeting; the house where one goes to meet God.

Then we turn from 1 Samuel 2 to Luke 2. What makes the story about Jesus so remarkable is that here he is, in the house where one goes to meet God. And he is determined to learn the law; to ask questions and to demonstrate his obedience to God. And one more thing. To his father-figure, he says "didn't you know I must be in my Father's house, about my father's business, involved in my father's work?"

Application

We must stop telling ourselves, "I can never live like Jesus." The gospel writers tell us that Jesus came in the spirit of those who have gone before, getting it better, getting it right. But Jesus serves as our example precisely because he answers the same call that was given to us long ago. The call to David to be God's man even in the face of betrayal; the call to John the Baptizer, to be God's servant, even in the face of mortal danger; the call to Moses, to be God's instrument, even in the face of seemingly insurmountable odds. He lived like us, so that we might live like him.

How did Jesus grow in favor with God?

Two ways: First, he claimed God as his father (or more correctly, he acknowledged God's claim on him to be God's son). Just read Proverbs 3:4, a proverb addressed from a father to "my child." Do you want to find favor and good repute in the sight of God and all the people? Then read verse 5: "Trust in the Lord with all your heart, and do not rely on your own insight; in all your ways *acknowledge Him*, and he will make straight your paths."

He was at peace with God's voice as the only voice to hear; God's will as the only will to seek. Can you imagine being so in tune with the Father? Lewis claimed the highest prayers are those that ask for nothing! "To be in the state which you are so at one with the will of God that you wouldn't want to alter the course of events even if you could!" [2]

Second, he did the seeking. He did his father's bidding; he studied and served; he labored and loved; he welcomed truth and avoided evil; he ministered faithfully and ran from temptation. He did what he was told. That is how you can identify the true son; just as the true "neighbor" is the one who acts neighborly, the son of God obeys dutifully the voice of his father. And Jesus grows in favor with God.

So, what does the boy Samuel have to do with the boy Jesus? For the Bible authors—both old and new—the heroes of the faith progressed in favor with God the way we all are called to progress in favor with God: by living virtuously, choosing wisely, acting without self-interest, in obedience to our father, whom he acknowledged as the one and only one who controls our lives.

Jesus also acted in self-sacrificial, God-focused obedience. He did what he was told…for the good of others, even when it was hard. He progressed in virtue, in an upward journey toward perfection. We know this because the word "favor" here carries the idea of reciprocity and social obligation. In Luke's larger storyline, the idea of patronage is prominent: a person wins over or curries

---

[2] C. S. Lewis, "Work and Prayer." In *God in the Dock* (1996), 104.

favor from his boss, his leader, or his father. In return, the one in charge offers grace, benevolence, and goodwill. Is it hard for us to think of Jesus "winning" God's respect? According to Luke, Jesus' mother Mary faces her unexpected pregnancy with a self-sacrificial resolve. Denying her own self-interest, she accepts the angelic message. In return, says Luke, Mary is called "highly favored one" (Luke 1:30). Luke says that the apostles in Jerusalem (Acts 2:47) experienced the "favor" of God and all the people because they sold all they had and gave it to the needy; and there was no poor among them. In each case, the hero mentioned acted according to God's will even when it might have gone against personal interest. For Luke, the lowly servant wins respect by choosing virtue, taking the high road, serving the needs of others, growing in knowledge and spiritual fruit. In fact, to really push the point that hard work, diligent study, and decisive action are involved, Luke even uses this word "favor" in places where the best translation is "gaining credit" from God and from other people. Just think of Jesus' message in his sermon on the plain: if you only love those who love you, do good to those who do good to you, or lend to those who lend to you, what credit is that to you? Instead, act virtuously...do the right thing, self-sacrificially, and your reward shall be great (Luke 6:32-36; Acts 7:10. Cf. 1 Pet 2:19-20).

The sense of benefaction, winning favor, earning credit, and acting not out of self-interest in deference to social obligation all combine to add a sense of living virtuously and actively acquiring virtues through active obedience which requires service/sacrifice.

So, for Luke, Jesus progressed in favor with God the way we all are called to progress in favor with God: by living virtuously, choosing wisely, acting without self-interest, in obedience to our father, who he acknowledged as the one and only one who controls our lives. And the writer of Hebrews confirms this when he says of Jesus, "Although he was a Son, he learned obedience through what he suffered; and having been made perfect, he became the source of eternal salvation for all who obey him" (Heb 5:8–9).

Maybe you have a hard time with this idea—winning God's respect through doing what's right. Perhaps you had a difficult father, for whom your deeds were never good enough; or perhaps you had a mother who never seemed pleased with you. No matter what you did. No matter how hard you tried.

Maybe the idea is difficult because it sounds so wrong. Loving Youth ministers have told you since you were little, every time you messed up: "What you did doesn't change God's view of you. God couldn't love you any more than he does right now, and no amount of good deeds can ever win his love. He loves you just the way you are." Yes. That's true. So how do we square that truth with this truth?

It helps to remember verse 40, which comes before the Temple scene. Before we are told of the boy Jesus living dutifully in the presence of God, we are told that the boy Jesus grew and became strong…and the favor of God was upon him. And that's not just true with Jesus. It's true with you as well. The boy Samuel, before we see his deeds in comparison with Eli's wicked sons, is introduced this way: "the boy Samuel grew up in the presence of the Lord." God's love for you, his calling on you, his acceptance of you is by his grace. He adopted you as his child before you had anything to offer him. And the Samuel story—between the bookends—gives us rich insight here. Eli, brooding over his sons, cries out, "If one man sins against another, God will judge him. But if a man sins against the Lord, who will intercede for Him?" Enter Jesus, at God's initiative, to intercede for us. Which we neither earned nor deserve.

Conclusion

But unlike getting taller or older, growing in wisdom involves decision and action. And growing in favor with God includes our decision to become what God has called us to be. We are right to sing "just as I am"; our father takes us just as we are. But his desire, his calling and his will is for us to progress. To advance. To grow. And whether we choose to develop virtues of character through sustained, disciplined, self-sacrificial obedience, can make the difference whether, when we are dead and gone, others tell our story as wicked sons standing in the doorway rejecting our father, or those who acknowledged our calling. May it be said on that day that you were one who not only stood but grew in favor with God.

Discussion Questions

1. What connections do you see between the story of Samuel and the story of Jesus?

2. Do you find it difficult to think about Jesus growing in wisdom and favor, the way Luke 2:52 says?

3. How do you think Samuel's childhood contributed to the faithful example he came to embody? Do you think aspects of his childhood were particularly difficult for him?

4. What parts of Samuel's story do you find most helpful to you as you grow in the life of faith. Faith is the foundation of our lives, directed toward a hoped-for future, trusting in the God who rewards believers.

Scripture Index

Old Testament

Genesis

1	87	12:6–7	29	22:12	32
3:1	40	15:6	6, 11	37–50	44, 47, 48
3:17	16	15:13–15	46	37:10	50
4:17	17	16	36	37:20–23	49
5:21–24	13	16:2	37	37:35	50
6	23	16:5	37	39	47
6–8	20	17–18	37	39:1	49
6–8n	21	17:16	37	39:9	48
6:5–9	13, 20	17:17	38	40:8	48
6:8	19	17:18	38	40:15	50
6:9	20	18:1	38	41:14	50
12	29, 31, 50, 59	18:15	38	41:16	49
12–21	36	21	32, 38	41:25	49
12:1	29	21:1	38	41:33–36	48
12:1–3	36, 48	21:6	39	41:39	49
		21:8ff	40	42:18	49
		22	31, 32, 34	42:28	49
		22:2	32		

42:38	50	2:5–10	53	12:1–8	55
44:18	50	2:11–12	53	12:7–8	55
44:20	50	3:10	55	14	54
44:30–33	50	14:31	54	18:13	54
45:5	47	18:1-27	55	**Deuteronomy**	
45:7	47	18:13	55	30:15–20	17
45:8	47, 50	25:1–40:38	56	32:35	49
45:9	49, 50	32:7–14	54	34:5	55
46:30	50	32:10–11	54	**Joshua**	
50:15	49	32:12–13	54	2:1–21	59
50:17	49	32:30–34	54	2:4–6	62
50:18	50	32:32	54	2:8–9	90
50:19	49	33:12–19	52	2:11	63
50:20	48, 49, 50	33:17–23	52	2:22	61
		34:6	52	2:24	61
50:24	50	**Numbers**		2:25	64
50:25	43, 46, 51	6	88	6:15–25	
Exodus		11:10–15	55	**Judges**	59
1:8	52	11:17	55	1:28	75
1:22	52	11:17–20	55	2:11–12	75
		11:25	55		

3:4	75	13–16	88	2:26	95
4	67, 68	14–16	88	12:11	70
4:4	68	14:2–3	88	17	11
4:6–7	68	14:5–9	88	**Psalms**	
4:8	69	14:6	88	28:1	49
4:20	69	14:14	88	30:3	49
5	70	14:15–17	88	88:4	49
6	75, 77	14:19	88	106:23	55
6:6	75	15:4–5	88	**Proverbs**	
6:6–10	75	15:14	88	3:4	96
6:11–13	75	15:15–16	88	3:5	96
6:14–16	76	16:4	89	31	87
6:20–21	76	16:5–14	89	**Isaiah**	
6:22–24	76	16:17	89	14:15	49
6:25–27	76	16:20	88	38:18	49
6:36–40	77	16:21	89	**Jeremiah**	
7:2	77	16:23–25	89	7:31	32
7:9–14	77	**1 Samuel**		**Habakkuk**	
7:15	77	2	95, 96	2:3–4	9
13	88	2:21	95	2:4	6

New Testament

Matthew
- 1:5–6 — 61
- 6:25–34 — 3
- 7:13–14 — 35
- 14:31 — 41
- 16:24–26 — 30
- 19:7–9 — 55

Mark
- 10 — 30
- 13 — 84

Luke
- 1:30 — 98
- 2 — 95, 96
- 2:40 — 95, 99
- 2:52 — 95, 100
- 6:32–36 — 98

John
- 3:16 — 11

Acts
- 2 — 87
- 2:39 — 57
- 2:47 — 98
- 4:13 — 78
- 4:29 — 78
- 7:10 — 98
- 7:22 — 53
- 10:23–24 — 64
- 10:23–38 — 66

Romans
- 1:17 — 9
- 3:24 — 64
- 4 — 11
- 6 — 51
- 15:4 — 56

1 Corinthians
- 10:11 — 51, 56
- 13 — 87

2 Corinthians
- 5:7 — 35
- 5:17 — 51

Galatians
- 3 — 11
- 3:11 — 9
- 3:26–27 — 64
- 5:23 — 40

Ephesians
- 6:1–4 — 64

Colossians
- 1:21–23 — 64
- 3:12 — 40

2 Thessalonians
- 3:9 — 57

1 Timothy
- 4:12 — 57

Hebrews
- 2:17 — 5
- 3:2 — 5
- 3:5 — 5
- 4:2n — 5

4:3	5	10:38n	5	11:13–16	30
5:7	22	10:39	9	11:13–19	28
5:8–9	99	10:39n	5	11:19	33
6:1n	5	11	4, 5, 9, 10, 11, 12, 20, 21, 23, 28, 29, 32, 34, 35, 44, 61, 68, 79, 87, 88, 89	11:22	36, 43, 44, 45
6:4	50			11:23	52, 53
6:11	41			11:24–25	53
6:12	40			11:26	53
6:12n	5	11n	21	11:30	11
6:16–17	41	11:1	6, 8, 11, 22, 29, 34	11:31	59, 61
10	12, 91			11:32	11, 67, 87, 93
10:5–10	91	11:1–2	90		
10:19–23	91	11:1–3	45, 51	11:32–34	74
10:22	41	11:3	22	11:34	74
10:22n	5	11:5	13	11:36–40	81
10:23	5	11:6	5, 8, 91	11:37	83
10:30	49	11:7	19, 21	12	28, 92
10:32	9	11:8	26, 29, 36	12:1	91
10:33–34	9	11:8–10	28, 29	12:1–2	35
10:35–39	91	11:11	5, 35, 36, 40	12:2	8, 10
10:36	9, 28			12:2n	5
10:38	6	11:13	10		

12:4	85	**1 Peter**		16	16
13:7n	5	1:1–7	85	19	16
13:22n	20	**2 Peter**		**Revelation**	
James		2:5	23	2:10–13	85
1:17	56	2:19–20	98	6:9–11	85, 86
2:18–26	64	**Jude**		20:4	85, 86
2:23	33	3–13	15–16		
2:24–25	59	14	14		

Contributors

Jeremy Barrier (PhD Brite Divinity School, Texas Christian University) is Associate Professor of Biblical Literature at HCU.

Jeffrey Brothers (MA University of North Alabama) is Instructor of Counseling at HCU.

Kirk Brothers (PhD Southern Baptist Theological Seminary) is President of HCU.

Nathan Daily (PhD in progress Claremont Graduate University) is Associate Professor of Religion at HCU.

Arvy Dupuy (MA Amridge University) is Adjunct Instructor at HCU.

Ed Gallagher (PhD Hebrew Union College) is Associate Professor of Christian Scripture at HCU.

Philip Goad is an alumnus of HCU (BA '11) and serves as HCU's Director of Alumni Relations.

Justin Guin (MMin Freed-Hardeman University) is Adjunct Instructor at HCU.

Nathan Guy (PhD Oxford University) is President of Mars Hill Bible School and adjunct professor at HCU.

Travis Harmon (MMin Heritage Christian University) is Director of Student Services and Instructor of Ministry at HCU.

Michael Jackson (EdD Union University) is Vice President of Academic Affairs and Associate Professor of Education and New Testament at HCU.

C. Wayne Kilpatrick (MAR Harding School of Theology) is Professor of Church History at HCU.

Brad McKinnon (MMin Freed-Hardman University; MA University of North Alabama; PhD in Progress University of Aberdeen) is Associate Professor of History and Director of Field Education at HCU.

CREDITS

Select Scripture quotations are taken from the NEW AMERICAN STANDARD BIBLE®, copyright© 1960, 1962, 1963, 1968, 1971,1972, 1973, 1975, 1977, 1995 by The Lockman Foundation. Used by permission.

Select Scripture quotations are taken from the NEW KING JAMES VERSION®. Copyright© 1982 by Thomas Nelson, Inc. Used by permission. All rights reserved.

Select Scripture quotations are taken from the NEW REVISED STANDARD VERSION BIBLE, copyright © 1989 National Council of the Churches of Christ in the United States of America. Used by permission. All rights reserved worldwide.

Select Scriptures quotations are taken from the Holy Bible, New International Version®, NIV®. Copyright © 1973, 1978, 1984, 2011 by Biblica, Inc.™ Used by permission of Zondervan. All rights reserved worldwide. www.zondervan.com The "NIV" and "New International Version" are trademarks registered in the United States Patent and Trademark Office by Biblica, Inc.®

Scripture quotations marked HCSB are been taken from the Holman Christian Standard Bible®, Copyright © 1999, 2000, 2002, 2003 by Holman Bible Publishers. Used by permission. Holman Christian Standard Bible®, Holman CSB®, and HCSB® are federally registered trademarks of Holman Bible Publishers.

www.ingramcontent.com/pod-product-compliance
Lightning Source LLC
Chambersburg PA
CBHW071005080526
44587CB00015B/2353